Cascadia

Cascadia

Library of Congress Control Number: 2013950834
ISBN 13: 978-1-937513-33-7
First Edition
Published by Cooperative Press
http://www.cooperativepress.com

Patterns, charts, schematics, and text © 2013,
Amanda Milne, Fiona McLean, and respective designers
Photography © 2013, Alexa Ludeman
Models: Brie, Jennifer and Sabrina Wood, Amanda Kaffka,
Chantelle Laviolette, Pat Ludeman, Jane Richmond, Emma Galati,
Sally Rudolf, Sebastian Lippa

For Cooperative Press

Senior Editor: Shannon Okey
Art Director and Assistant Editor: Elizabeth Green Musselman
Technical Editor: Kate Atherley
Copy Editor: Kim Werker

For our community of knitters,
both near and far.

Contents

Foreword by Kim Werker 7
Introduction by Knit Social 9

Beacon Hill
by Jane Richmond

13

Meet Jane Richmond 10
Sweet Fiber Yarns Feature 16

Britannia
by Tin Can Knits

23

Meet Tin Can Knits 20
SweetGeorgia Yarns Feature 25

Redcedar
by Emily Wessel

31

Everything Old Feature 33

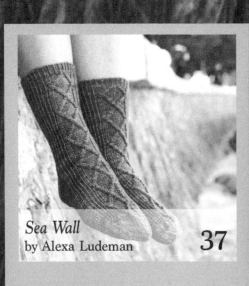

Sea Wall
by Alexa Ludeman

37

Courtenay
by Megan Goodacre

43

Meet Megan Goodacre 40

Raven's Nest
by Judy Marples

53

Meet Judy Marples 50

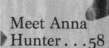

Meet Anna
Hunter . . . 58

Wake
by Holli Yeoh

63

Meet Holli Yeoh 60

Wickaninnish
by Holli Yeoh

71

Kattikloo Feature 73

Tidal Flats
by Melissa Thomson

81

Meet Melissa Thomson 78

Sea Glass
by Amanda Kaffka

91

Meet Amanda Kaffka 88

Meet Caitlin
ffrench 86

Heather
by Amanda Milne

101

Meet Amanda Milne 98
Indigo Moon Feature 103

Abbreviations & Resources 106
Acknowledgments 107
About Knit Social 108
About Cooperative Press 109

Foreword

I'M NOT FROM THE PACIFIC NORTHWEST, I JUST CHOOSE TO LIVE HERE. Most mornings, I leave my city home and walk the dog three blocks to the west, into the woods. At each intersection we cross on our way, I never fail to glance north, hoping the clouds will allow me a view of the mountains. Oh, the mountains. So close, they colour my every day.

On the south coast of British Columbia, the dramatic natural setting is as much a part of daily life as brushing your teeth and walking the dog. But somehow, it never fades into the background. It never becomes the ubiquitous thing that's taken for granted. The massive trees, calm waters and mountains define this place, and seep into our subconscious, eventually to get churned into the conversations we have, the activities we enjoy, the things we make.

In the fall of 2012, when Amanda and Fiona held the first Knit City event in Vancouver, they accomplished something I'd only dreamed of for our city – lines of knitters snaking out the door, people talking with strangers about what was on their needles. They'd invited me – a crocheter! – to speak at the kick-off party, and the conversations I had afterward with perfect strangers were inspiring. I felt the magic that weekend, in no small part because I felt a part of my city in a way I never had before. I felt a part of something. I felt I was with my people.

That's the beauty of what Amanda and Fiona do: They bring people together in a celebration of shared craft, within a beloved setting that never fails to inspire. This book is a concrete version of what they do through their events. It's a collection of individual voices and styles that combine into a celebration of community and place. A celebration that's intended to be shared.

— *Kim Werker | August 2013 | Vancouver, BC*

Introduction

WE LIVE IN CASCADIA: THE MYTHICAL SOUNDING TEMPERATE REGION bordering the west coast of Canada and the northern United States, and defined by the Cascades mountain range. It is synonymous with the strikingly beautiful contours of our West Coast landscape: the mountains, rainforests, ocean and beaches we have such easy access to. This area is perfect for knitting year-round, and our predictable weather (rain, more rain, mild summers and winters) is ideal for showing off our hand-knits, or at least having one tucked away in our bags, just in case.

We are both native British Columbians; having grown up surrounded by mountains and water has continually inspired us and shaped our creative sensibilities. Since we began Knit Social, a knit-centric events company, in 2011, we have been fortunate to meet and work alongside many talented knitwear designers and yarn dyers from our local fibre community. Bringing these talents together and pairing them with outstanding photography has created something we are truly proud of. Each of the patterns that we have selected for this book has a Cascadian story behind it: an inspiration, a childhood memory, a home town – something that makes it locally unique.

This book is an homage to our home, and a celebration of the talent that lies here. We hope you enjoy it.

Happy knitting,
Amanda & Fiona

Meet Jane Richmond

W E HAVE ONLY KNOWN JANE RICHMOND PERSONALLY FOR ABOUT A YEAR, BUT we've certainly known *of* her for much longer due to her huge following on Ravelry. We are big fans of hers (her Child's Classic Raglan was one of my first knitting projects) and long-time admirers of her simple, classic designs, eye for detail, and dedication to clearly written patterns. Jane lives a ferry ride away from us in Victoria, on nearby Vancouver Island, a place that is very inspirational to her and has greatly influenced her design work. We are proud to call her a friend and associate and couldn't imagine Cascadia without a design from her. —*Fiona*

Where were you born? How long have you lived in BC? What brought you here if you weren't born or raised here?

I am from BC and have lived here off and on. I was born in Victoria, on Vancouver Island, and was adopted to parents from mainland Vancouver. At age 10, my father's job landed us as expatriates in Melbourne, Australia; then Seoul, South Korea; and eventually Pittsburgh, Pennsylvania, where I went on to graduate high school. My sister and I then returned to Canada, landing in Victoria rather than Vancouver. I love the Island, it is home to me, and I feel like I've unintentionally come full circle, back to the place where I was born.

What was the catalyst that took you from knitting to design? What did you do prior to this or what do you in addition to this as an occupation?

Knitting made a huge resurgence in my life when I was pregnant with my daughter Elsie. Being at home after she was born was how I found myself designing. While on maternity leave I was no longer leaving the home to go to my day job and found that really isolating, which lead me to reach out to local knitting groups through the internet and especially Ravelry. The encouragement of these amazing friends is what pushed me over the threshold of knitwear design.

I've worn many hats in search of a job that fueled my need to be hands-on. At one point I was training to become an auto mechanic – it fulfilled my need to work hard, be hands on, and problem solve but certainly wasn't a creative outlet. After my daughter was born and my maternity leave was up, I took a job at Costco to supplement my design income. Once my business was established

enough to support me, I made the decision to leave and design full-time.

What is your favourite part of your job?

This is my dream job and there is an endless list of things I love about it. I think for me, being able to be creative in my career is a dream come true. It's as though I'd been missing something; I feel very fulfilled and truly grateful to be able to do this for a living.

Tell us about your design process.

Typically I design with a sketch or concept in mind. Then comes the search for the perfect yarn, which can be quite difficult depending on how specific my ideas are.

Perfect yarn in hand, I move on to swatching different design elements. Once I have a good idea of what will and won't work, I hunker down and produce a spreadsheet to base the pattern on. I then use the raw numbers to write up the pattern. I like to produce a final copy of the written pattern so that I can have the same experience as the knitter while I knit my sample. This is where I can really hone in on trouble spots or portions of the pattern that could be clearer or simplified.

The pattern then gets tested by knitters and reviewed by a technical editor. During this time the piece will be photographed and the layout will be finalized.

Tell us about your most epic knitting disaster.

While I was pregnant I knit this adorable and elaborate hooded cardigan for Elsie. I knew in my heart of hearts that she would have red hair so I chose this gorgeous grassy green colour. I resisted the temptation to make it teeny tiny and instead opted for the two-year

size that might get more use. It was a labour of love and the end result was stunning. The only issue was the hood: it was big enough to fit an adult. I tucked it away and decided to worry about it later.

Well, later turned into two-and-a-half years, and with Elsie pushing two, I set out to fix the hood. But I had done an incredible job burying my ends and I couldn't find them anywhere. I kept pulling the knitted fabric this way and that hoping to find some evidence of the woven in ends. Eventually I decided to poke around with a pair of scissors.... I bet you know where this is going. I ended up cutting into a stitch (or two) and the entire neck edge threatened to unravel. It was a mess, and I still hadn't uncovered my ends. Elsie is now five and the sweater lives in permanent hibernation.

Favourite recent project?

To be honest? My favourite recent project would have to be my cardigan for Cascadia. It's far more elaborate than the garments I normally design because of the all-over stitch pattern and shaped collar. I had never designed a shawl collar before and had a very specific idea of how I wanted it to look, it took an amazing amount of trial and error to achieve the desired fullness and height. I feel very attached to this design now that it's finished, it is exactly what I set out to create.

Beacon Hill

Jane Richmond

THIS DESIGN BEGAN AS A STITCH PATTERN RATHER than an idea for a garment. I was playing with a combination of stitches, trying to create a fabric reminiscent of the raindrops that represent our West Coast winters. My original submission became what is now the published Wellington hat. Amanda and Fiona, loving the raindrop pattern stitch, asked if I could design a garment with it.

I set out to create a cozy, grandfather-type cardigan with a long body and sleeves for a sweater you could live in. Pairing this silhouette with the luminescent qualities of Sweet Fiber's neutral colourway Paper Birch resulted in a finished garment that literally gleams as raindrops would.

About the Designer

Jane lives and works from her home on Vancouver Island. She has been self-publishing her designs since 2008, and most recently published her first book, ISLAND. Known for her classic aesthetic and clearly written patterns, Jane delivers designs that are fun to knit and easy to wear.

REQUIRED SKILLS

Basic knitting skills; knitting in the round; knitting with double-pointed needles; backward loop cast on; twisted stitches; slipped stitches; knit-on edging; knowledge of basic sweater construction; picking up stitches; seaming; sewing on buttons

SIZES

30 (34, 36, 40, 42, 44, 48, 50)" bust, shown in size 34 with 2" of negative ease.

FINISHED MEASUREMENTS

Bust: 28 (32, 34, 38, 40, 42, 46, 48)"

Garment Length: 23½ (23¾, 24¼, 24¼, 24½, 24¾, 24¾, 25)"

MATERIALS

Sweet Fiber Merino Twist Worsted (100% superwash merino; 200yds/183m per 115g skein); color: Paper Birch; 6 (7, 7, 8, 8, 8, 9, 10) skeins

32-inch US #6/4mm circular needle, or size needed to obtain gauge.

1 set US #6/4mm double-point needles, or preferred method for working small circumference in the rnd

4 stitch markers
8 × 1⅛-inch buttons
Stitch holders or waste yarn for sleeve sts
Yarn needle

GAUGE

21 sts and 27 rows = 4"/10 cm in pattern stitch (blocked)

Both stitch gauge and row gauge are important – please check your gauge carefully!

19 sts and 26 rows = 4"/10 cm in St st (unblocked)

PATTERN NOTES

This cardigan is knit from the top down in an all-over stitch pattern created by alternating left and right twists. The collar is picked up gradually to add shaping and height, and double thickness creates a wonderfully full shawl collar, cementing the cornerstone of this look.

STITCHES AND TECHNIQUES

Kfb: Knit into the front and back of the st; 2 sts made from 1.

LT: Insert RH needle into back of second st on LH needle and knit st through back lp, leave st on needle, k2tog tbl.

RT: K2tog leaving sts on needle, knit first st, slip both sts off of needle.

LT inc: Insert RH needle into back of second st on LH needle and knit st through back lp, leave st on needle, k2tog tbl leaving the sts on the needle, knit through the front of the first st and slip all 3 sts off of needle.

RT inc: K2tog leaving sts on needle, knit through front and back of first st, slip all 3 sts off of needle.

One-Row Buttonhole: Bring yarn to front and sl 1 purlwise, bring yarn to the back, *sl 1 from LH needle, pass the 2nd st on the RH needle over the last st and off the needle, rep from * 3 more times, slip last bound off st to LH needle and turn work, CO 5 sts using the cable cast on method, turn work, with yarn in back, slip the first st from LH needle to RH needle and pass the last CO st over it and off the needle.

m1: Insert LH needle from front to back under the horizontal bar between the two needles, knit through the back of the lifted st.

PATTERN

Yoke

Using long-tail method, CO 52 (52, 56, 56, 56, 60, 60, 60) sts.

Row 1 (Set-Up Row) (WS): P1 front st, pm, p10 sleeve sts, pm, p30 (30, 34, 34, 34, 38, 38, 38) back sts, pm, p10 sleeve sts, pm, p1 front st.

Row 2 (RS): Kfb, sm, kfb,*[LT, RT] to last st before marker, kfb, sm, kfb, rep from * twice more. 8 sts inc'd.
Row 3 and every following WS Row: Purl.

Row 4: [Knit to 1 st before marker, kfb, sm, kfb] 3 more times, knit to end of row. 8 sts inc'd.

Row 6: Kfb, k1, kfb, sm, kfb, *[LT, RT] to last st before marker, kfb, sm, kfb, rep from * twice more, k1, kfb. 10 sts inc'd.

Row 8: Rep Row 4.
Row 10: Kfb, LT, RT, kfb, sm, kfb, *[LT, RT] to last st before marker, kfb, sm, kfb, rep from * twice more, LT, RT, kfb. 10 sts inc'd.

Row 12: Rep Row 4.
Row 14: Kfb, k1, RT, LT, RT, kfb, sm, kfb, *[LT, RT] to last st before marker, kfb, sm, kfb, rep from * twice more, LT, RT, LT, k1, kfb. 10 sts inc'd.

Row 16: Rep Row 4.
Row 18: Kfb, RT, [LT, RT] to last st before marker, kfb, sm, kfb, *[LT, RT] to last st before marker, kfb, sm, kfb, rep from * twice more, [LT, RT] to last 3 sts, LT, kfb. 10 sts inc'd.

Row 20: Rep Row 4.
Row 22: Kfb, k1, [LT, RT] to last st before marker, kfb, sm, kfb, *[LT, RT] to last st before marker, kfb,

sm, kfb, rep from * twice more, [LT, RT] to last 2 sts, k1, kfb. 10 sts inc'd.

Row 24: Rep Row 4.
Row 26: Kfb, [LT, RT] to last st before marker, kfb, sm, kfb, *[LT, RT] to last st before marker, kfb, sm, kfb, rep from * twice more, [LT, RT] to last st, kfb. 10 sts inc'd.

Row 28: Rep Row 4.
Row 30: Kfb, k1, RT, [LT, RT] to last st before marker, kfb, sm, kfb, *[LT, RT] to last st before marker, kfb, sm, kfb, rep from * twice more, [LT, RT] to last 4 sts, LT, k1, kfb. 10 sts inc'd.

Row 32: Rep Row 4.
Row 33: Purl.

IMPORTANT: READ AHEAD BEFORE PROCEEDING. Rep Rows 18–33 while observing the st counts outlined below for each section:

Sleeves

Once there are 48 (52, 56, 56, 60, 60, 68, 72) sts per sleeve, work even in st pattern on the sleeve sts as required until back increases are complete.

Fronts

Once there are 29 (33, 35, 41, 43, 45, 49, 53) sts per front section, stop neck and raglan increases in front section, work those sections even in st pattern as required until back increases are complete.

Sizes 34, 42, 44, 48 only: The last front shaping row is slightly modified, place inc as foll:

- *Sizes 34 & 44*: Place inc at neck edge rather than sleeve marker for Row 28.

- *Size 42*: Inc at sleeve marker only, omit inc at neck edge, for Row 26.

- *Size 48*: Inc at sleeve marker only, omit inc at neck edge, for Row 18.

Back

All sizes: Once there are 68 (72, 80, 88, 92, 96, 104, 108) back sts, work even in st pattern as est without increasing (kfb).

Complete the yoke as follows: Work even in patt for 5 (7, 5, 5, 5, 3, 5, 5) more rows.
29 (33, 35, 41, 43, 45, 49, 53) front sts per side, 48 (52, 56, 56, 60, 60, 68, 72) sts for each sleeve, 68 (72, 80, 88, 92, 96, 104, 108) back sts. 222 (242, 262, 282, 298, 306, 338, 358) total yoke sts.

Separate sleeves from body as follows:
Next Row: Knit to marker, remove marker, place 48 (52, 56, 56, 60, 60, 68, 72) sleeve sts onto waste yarn, remove marker, CO 2 (6, 4, 6, 4, 6, 6, 6), pm, CO 6 (6, 8, 6, 8, 6, 10, 10), knit to marker, remove marker, place 48 (52, 56, 56, 60, 60, 68, 72) sleeve sts onto waste yarn, remove marker, CO 6 (6, 8, 6, 8, 6, 10, 10), pm, CO 2 (6, 4, 6, 4, 6, 6, 6), knit to end of row. 142 (162, 174, 194, 202, 210, 234, 246) total body sts.

Lower Body

Next Row: Purl.

Sizes 34, 36, 42 only:
Row 1: K1, [LT, RT] to last st, k1.
Rows 2–4: Work in St st.
Row 5: K1, [RT, LT] to last st, k1.
Rows 6–8: Work in St st.

Sizes 30, 40, 44, 48, 50 only:
Row 1: K1, [RT, LT] to last st, k1.
Row 2–4: Work in St st.
Row 5: K1, [LT, RT] to last st, k1.
Rows 6–8: Work in St st.

All sizes: Work even in patt as set until cardigan measures approx 7¾ (7½, 7¾, 7, 6¼, 6¼, 6, 6)" from CO at underarm, ending with Row 4 (8, 8, 4, 8, 4, 4, 4).

Waist Shaping

Row 1: K1, *[LT, RT] to 2 sts before marker, ssk, sm, k2tog, rep from * once more, [LT, RT] to last st, k1. 138 (158, 170, 190, 198, 206, 230, 242) sts.
Rows 2-4: Work in St st.

Row 5: K1, *[RT, LT] to last st before marker, k1, sm, k1, rep from * once more, [RT, LT] to last st, k1.
Rows 6-8: Work in St st.

Row 9: K1, LT, [RT, LT] to last 3 sts before marker, k2tog, k1, sm, k1, ssk, [RT, LT] to last 3 sts before marker, k2tog, k1, sm, k1, ssk, [RT, LT] to last 3 sts of row, RT, k1. 134 (154, 166, 186, 194, 202, 226, 238) sts.

Work Even

Rows 1-3: Work in St st.
Row 4: K1, [RT, LT] to last st, k1.
Rows 5-7: Work in St st.
Row 8: K1, [LT, RT] to last st, k1.
Work Rows 1-7 once more.

Hip Shaping

Row 1: K1, [LT, RT] to 2 sts before marker, RT inc, sm, m1, LT, [RT, LT] to 2 sts before marker, RT inc, sm, m1, [LT, RT] to last st, k1. 138 (158, 170, 190, 198, 206, 214, 238, 254) sts.
Rows 2-4: Work in St st.

Row 5: K1, *[RT, LT] to last st before marker, k1, sm, k1, rep from * once more, [RT, LT] to last st, k1.
Rows 6-8: Work in St st.

Row 9: K1, *[LT, RT] to last st before marker, m1, k1, sm, k1, m1, rep from * once more, [LT, RT] to last st, k1. 142 (162, 174, 194, 202, 210, 234, 250) sts.
Rows 10-12: Work in St st.

Row 13: K1, *[RT, LT] to last st, k1.
Rows 14-16: Work in St st.

Row 17: K1, [LT, RT] to 2 sts before marker, LT inc, sm, m1, RT, [RT, LT] to last 2 sts before marker, LT inc, sm, m1, RT, [LT, RT] to last st, k1. 146 (166, 178, 198, 206, 214, 238, 254) sts.
Rows 18-20: Work in St st.

Row 21: K1, RT, *[LT, RT] to last st before marker, k1, sm, k1, rep from * once more, LT, [RT, LT] to last st, k1.
Rows 22-24: Work in St st.

Row 25: K1, LT, *[RT, LT] to last st before marker, m1, k1, remove marker, k1, m1, rep from * once more, RT, [LT, RT] to last st, k1. 150 (170, 182, 202, 210, 218, 242, 254) sts.

Ribbing

Next Row (WS): [K2, p2] to last 2 sts, k2.

Next Row (RS): [P2, k2] to last 2 sts, p2. Rep last 2 rows until ribbing measures 2". BO in rib.

Sleeves

Return 48 (52, 56, 56, 60, 60, 68, 72) sleeve sts to needles for working in the rnd. Rejoin yarn and with RS facing, starting at CO sts, pick up and knit 8 (12, 12, 12, 12, 12, 16, 16) sts along CO edge of underarm, placing a marker at centre of picked up sts to denote beg of rnd. Join. 56 (64, 68, 68, 72, 72, 84, 88) total sleeve sts.

Knit 2 rnds.

Sizes 30, 36, 40, 42, 44, 48, 50 only:
Rnd 1: [RT, LT] to end of rnd.
Rnds 2-4: Knit.
Rnd 5: [LT, RT] to end of rnd.

Melissa Thomson & Sweet Fiber Yarns

Sweet Fiber Yarns is a luxury hand dyed yarn company located near Vancouver in British Columbia, Canada. With a background in painting and colour theory, and a BFA from the Emily Carr University of Art and Design, I understand the visual languages of design, presentation, form and colour. It is with this knowledge that I strive to supply today's knitters with incredible colourways, exquisite yarns, and unique knitwear designs.

My inspiration comes from the colour relationships I notice throughout my daily life. I make mental notes of how they look together, how they change beside one another and the conversations they create amongst one another. It is important to me that my colourways are not only a pleasure to knit but also entirely wearable. Experimenting and creating new colourways is one of my favourite parts about my job; that, and designing and knitting with the colours I make.

I love the entire process of knitting – the rhythm, the texture, the transformation of materials and the way it opens your mind and allows it to wander through thoughts and ideas you wouldn't otherwise have time for. Knitting is how I relax and unwind and I'm grateful that something so simple can bring me so much pleasure.

Rnds 6–8: Knit.

Size 34 only:
Rnd 1: [LT, RT] to end of rnd.
Rnds 2–4: Knit.
Rnd 5: [RT, LT] to end of rnd.
Rnds 6–8: Knit.

All sizes: Rep last 8 rnds until sleeve measures approx 10 (7¾, 5¾, 5¾, 5¼, 7¾, 1¾, 1¾)" from underarm, ending with Rnd 4 (8, 4, 4, 4, 4, 4, 4).

Sleeve Shaping

Rnd 1: Ssk, [RT, LT] to last 2 sts of rnd, k2tog.
Rnds 2–4: Knit.
Rnd 5: K1, [LT, RT] to last st of rnd, k1.
Rnds 6–8: Knit.
Rnd 9: K1, k2tog, [LT, RT] to last 3 sts, ssk, k1.
Rnds 10–12: Knit.
Rnd 13: [LT, RT] to end of rnd.
Rnds 14–16: Knit.
Rnd 17: K2tog, [LT, RT] to last 2 sts, ssk.
Rnds 18–20: Knit.
Rnd 21: K1, [RT, LT] to last st of rnd, k1.
Rnds 22–24: Knit.
Rnd 25: K1, ssk, [RT, LT] to last 3 sts, k2tog, k1.
Rnds 26–28: Knit.
Rnd 29: [RT, LT] to end of rnd.
Rnds 30–32: Knit.

Rep from Rnds 1 until 44 (48, 48, 48, 52, 56, 56, 60) sleeve sts rem, ending with Rnd 16 (32, 16, 16, 16, 32, 16, 16).

Sizes 30, 36, 40, 42, 48, 50 only:
Next Rnd: [RT, LT] to end of rnd.
Next Rnd: K1, [p2, k2] to last 3 sts of rnd, p2, k1.

Sizes 34, 44 only:
Next Rnd: [LT, RT] to end of rnd.
Next Rnd: P1, [k2, p2] to last 3 sts of rnd, k2, p1.

All sizes: Rep last rnd until ribbing measures 2 in. BO loosely in rib.

Front Edgings

Right Band – Buttonhole band
With RS facing, beg at bottom right corner of front, pick up and knit 103 (103, 103, 99, 99, 95, 95, 91) sts.

Row 1 (WS): P3, [k2, p2] to end.
Row 2 (RS): [K2, p2] to last 3 sts, k3. Rep last 2 rows once more.

Next Row (Buttonhole Row): Work in rib for 4 (4, 4, 7, 7, 3, 3, 6) sts, work One-Row Buttonhole as described under Stitches and Techniques, *work in rib for 8 (8, 8, 7, 7, 7, 7, 6) sts, work One-Row Buttonhole, rep from * 6 more times, k1, p2.

Next Row (RS): [K2, p2] to last 3 sts, k3.
Next Row (WS): P3, [k2, p2] to end.
Rep last 2 rows once more, then RS row once more.
BO in rib.

Left Band – Button band
With RS facing, beg at top left front corner, at base of v-neck, pick up and knit 103 (103, 103, 99, 99, 95, 95, 91) sts.

Row 1 (WS): [P2, k2] to last 3 sts, p3.
Row 2 (RS): K3, [p2, k2] to end.
Rep last 2 rows 4 more times.
BO in rib.

Collar

With RS facing, pick up and knit 50 (50, 54, 54, 54, 58, 58, 58) sts along sleeves and back neck as foll: 10 sts along right sleeve, 30 (30, 34, 34, 34, 38, 38, 38) sts along back neck, 10 sts along left sleeve.

Row 1 (WS): P5 (5, 7, 7, 7, 9, 9, 9), [p1, kfb] to last 5 (5, 7, 7, 7, 9, 9, 9) sts, purl to end of row, pick up and knit 2 sts along the neck edge. 72 (72, 76, 76, 76, 80, 80, 80) sts.

Row 2 (RS): [K2, p2] to end, pick up and knit 2 sts along neck edge.

Row 3: P2, [k2, p2] to end, pick up and knit 2 sts along neck edge.

Row 4: [P2, k2] to end, pick up and knit 2 sts along neck edge.

Row 5: K2, [p2, k2] to end of row. Rep last 4 rows until the entire length of v-neck edge has been picked up (do not pick up along tops of buttonbands). Be mindful of the rate at which you are picking up to keep both sides even.

Approximately 158 (174, 178, 186, 186, 206, 206, 214) total collar sts. Work in rib as set for 22 rows.

Next Row: BO 2 sts, work in rib to end of row. Rep last row until 70 (70, 74, 74, 74, 78, 78, 78) sts rem. Next Row: K5 (5, 7, 7, 7, 9, 9, 9) sts, [k2tog, k1] to last 5 (5, 7, 7, 7, 9, 9, 9) sts, knit to end of row. 50 (50, 54, 54, 54, 58, 58, 58) sts. BO.

With WS facing, fold collar in half widthwise and align bound off edge with inside of picked up neck edge, seam in place.

Finishing

Sew buttons onto left front buttonband corresponding with buttonholes. Weave in ends. Wet block according to schematic measurements.

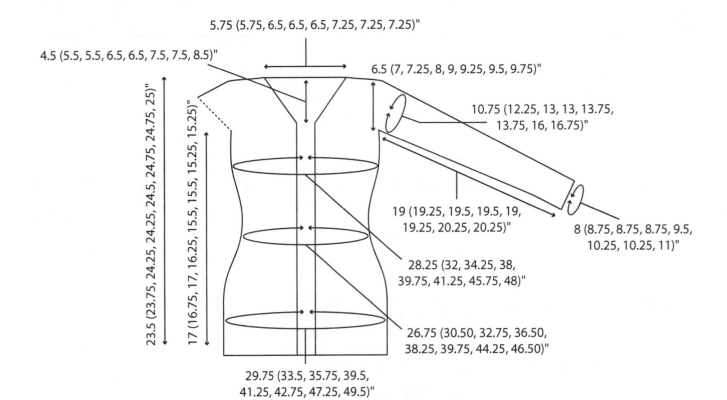

5.75 (5.75, 6.5, 6.5, 6.5, 7.25, 7.25, 7.25)"

4.5 (5.5, 5.5, 6.5, 6.5, 7.5, 7.5, 8.5)"

6.5 (7, 7.25, 8, 9, 9.25, 9.5, 9.75)"

10.75 (12.25, 13, 13, 13.75, 13.75, 16, 16.75)"

23.5 (23.75, 24.25, 24.25, 24.5, 24.75, 24.75, 25)"

17 (16.75, 17, 16.25, 15.5, 15.5, 15.25, 15.25)"

19 (19.25, 19.5, 19.5, 19, 19.25, 20.25, 20.25)"

8 (8.75, 8.75, 8.75, 9.5, 10.25, 10.25, 11)"

28.25 (32, 34.25, 38, 39.75, 41.25, 45.75, 48)"

26.75 (30.50, 32.75, 36.50, 38.25, 39.75, 44.25, 46.50)"

29.75 (33.5, 35.75, 39.5, 41.25, 42.75, 47.25, 49.5)"

Meet Tin Can Knits

ALEXA AND EMILY OF TIN CAN KNITS MET WHILE WORKING TOGETHER AT URBAN Yarns in Vancouver – which is where we first met them too, at the launch party for their first book, *9 Months of Knitting*. Since then, this duo has become an unstoppable force in the knitting world, with a near-constant release of beautiful and innovative patterns.

We feel a certain affinity for them and their business partnership, although they do trump us by living halfway around the world from each other! It's very inspiring to see collaboration work so well and so consistently, and we were thrilled to have Alexa and Emily be a part of Cascadia. —*Amanda and Fiona*

Where were you born? How long have you lived in BC? What brought you here if you weren't born or raised here?

Alexa: Born at Burnaby General. All my life!

Emily: I was born in Comox, on Vancouver Island. I grew up in BC, but have lived many places since then in Canada, in the US and abroad, in Edinburgh, UK. The coast holds a special place in my heart, and I get teary-eyed every time I fly into Vancouver and I see the ocean, mountains, and islands below me.

What is the most inspiring part of BC for you?

A: Probably Tofino, on Vancouver Island. I take a road trip to Tofino every year and I always come back feeling re-charged and re-inspired in many ways. I love the coast and the beautiful lush forests, as well as the hippy vibe!

E: I love Desolation Sound. As a child, my parents took my sister and me sailing and we explored narrow inlets, anchored in bays, and camped on tiny little islands. We had beach fires and went skinny dipping in the dark, and were blown away by the beauty of the phosphorescence (bioluminescence) of the plankton lighting up like stars in the black water.

Who taught you to knit?

A: I learned to knit from a 1970s stitchionary. I have rather odd/ terrible technique because of it; I throw with my left hand.

E: My mom and my aunt taught me knit and purl. (I made a terrible curling stockinette scarf or two). In university I needed a new way to procrastinate, so I picked up some needles and taught myself the rest!

What was the catalyst that took you from knitting to design? What did you do prior to this or what do you in addition to this as an occupation?

A: When I learned to knit I started by creating blankets. I would pick a stitch (from the aforementioned book) and create a six-foot scarf with a seed-stitch border. I would then sew them all together and *voila*, blanket! That's how I learned so many different stitches.

When I worked at Urban Yarns they were so supportive of their staff breaking into the design world, too. It seemed natural that knitters would write their own patterns!

E: My passion for design led me to study architecture, and I worked in that field until Alexa and I started Tin Can Knits in 2011. Almost as soon as I started knitting, I began to design. Whenever I work in a new medium, I immediately want to see what I can do with it, to explore the design possibilities. This means I am not a very good pattern follower!

Tell us about your design process.

A: People ask all the time where my design inspiration comes from but I don't have a very satisfying answer. I really draw inspiration from all over. I love the natural beauty and the varied culture of BC. When I think of a new design I also like to think about how I will photograph it. That may seem odd but it helps me think about what the design is all about. I also find inspiration in a texture, a stitch pattern, a garment construction. It seems that inspiration is everywhere to me.

The design process really depends on where I start. If I start with a stitch, the next question is what kind of knitted item will I make from that stitch? If it's a construction, the next step is which stitch? If the idea seems to come from thin air, there is a lot of work to be done!

E: My best ideas pop into my head at the oddest times and places – usually not when I'm consciously thinking about design. I was having coffee with an artist friend when the concept for the POP blanket 'popped' into my head, and I rushed home to figure out how to make it happen. I also have great ideas in the shower.

From a concept sketch I gather data – which possible stitch patterns, what yarn weight, what the gauge is in stockinette and over the stitch pattern.... Then the specifics of the pattern can be worked out, and the initial sample knit up. Often, a design doesn't work out the first time I knit it, so I have to revise and reknit until I get it right.

Tell us about the project you're most proud of.

A: The Antler sweater is my most proud project to date. It has been successfully knit by so many knitters, including one of my knitting idols, The Yarn Harlot.

E: I am very proud of my Low Tide cardigan. I designed the lace stitch pattern myself, and the biasing nature of the lace inspired me to use it in the bodice of a cardigan. It turned out even better than my initial vision, and looks adorable on all shapes and sizes!

What's the strangest place you've ever knit?

A: It's not strange to knit anywhere, is it?

E: This is embarrassing, but when I lived in Vancouver, I learned to knit whilst walking, and I would do this every morning while I walked to the bus I caught to work. I think that was a little bit extreme, even for me.

Britannia

Tin Can Knits

BRITANNIA COMBINES SIMPLE SWEATER CONSTRUCTION with cable and lace details, making it the perfect sweater for a walk on the beach or a drive down the Sea-to-Sky Highway.

REQUIRED SKILLS

Basic knitting skills; knitting in the round; knitting with double-pointed needles; increases; decreases; three-needle bind off; working simple cables/lace from charts; picking up stitches

SIZES

0–6 mo (6–12 mo, 1–2 yr, 2–4 yr, 4–6 yr, 6–8 yr, 8–10 yr, Ladies XS, S, M, L, XL, XXL, 3XL, 4XL)

FINISHED MEASUREMENTS

Chest: 18 (20, 22, 24, 26, 28, 30, 32, 36, 40, 44, 48, 52, 56, 60)"

Length from hem to underarm: 7 (8, 8½, 9½, 10, 13, 15, 15½, 16, 17, 18, 18½, 19, 20, 20)"

Sleeve length: 7½ (8, 9, 10½, 12, 14, 15, 18, 19, 19, 20, 20, 21, 21, 21)"

MATERIALS

320 (350, 400, 500, 600, 700, 800, 900, 1000, 1100, 1150, 1200, 1350, 1450, 1550) yds DK-weight yarn (samples shown in SweetGeorgia Superwash DK in Lettuce Wrap and Goldmine)

US #5/3.75mm 20–32-inch circular and double-pointed needles for hem and cuffs

US #7/4.5mm 20–32-inch circular and double pointed needles for body – or sizes needed to obtain gauge

Cable needle
Stitch markers

GAUGE

18 sts and 28 rnds = 4"/10cm in St st on larger needles after blocking

Cable width after blocking: child sizes: 3"; adult sizes: 4"

Lace panel width after blocking: child sizes: 2"; adult sizes: XS–L: 3", XL–4XL: 4".

PATTERN

Back and Front

With smaller needles CO 80 (88, 96, 108, 116, 124, 132, 136, 144, 160, 172, 184, 204, 220, 240) sts, pm and join for working in the rnd. Work 1 (1, 2, 2, 2, 2½, 2½, 2½, 2½, 3, 3, 3, 3, 3, 3)" in garter st (knit 1 rnd, purl 1 rnd). Switch to larger needles.

Cable set-up row: K2 (6, 6, 12, 16, 20, 24, 8, 12, 20, 26, 22, 32, 40, 50), pm, p1 (1, 2, 2, 2, 2, 2, 3, 3, 3, 3, 4, 4, 4, 4), k9 (9, 9, 9, 9, 9, 9, 9, 9, 12, 12, 12, 12, 15, 15, 15, 15), p1 (1, 2, 2, 2, 2, 2, 3, 3, 3, 3, 4, 4, 4, 4), (k2, m1) 8 (8, 8, 8, 8, 8, 8, 12, 12, 12, 12, 12, 12, 12, 12) times, p1 (1, 2, 2, 2, 2, 2, 3, 3, 3, 3, 4, 4, 4, 4), k9 (9, 9, 9, 9, 9, 9, 12, 12, 12, 12, 15, 15, 15, 15), p1 (1, 2, 2, 2, 2, 2, 3, 3, 3, 3, 4, 4, 4, 4), pm, twice.

96 (104, 112, 124, 132, 140, 148, 160, 168, 184, 196, 208, 228, 244, 264) sts.

Rnd 1: [Knit to marker, p1 (1, 2, 2, 2, 2, 3, 3, 3, 3, 4, 4, 4, 4), work Chart A, p1 (1, 2, 2, 2, 2, 2, 3, 3, 3, 3, 4, 4, 4, 4 work Chart B, p1 (1, 2, 2, 2, 2, 2, 3, 3, 3, 3, 4, 4, 4, 4), work Chart C, p1 (1, 2, 2, 2, 2, 2, 3, 3, 3, 3, 4, 4, 4, 4)] twice.

Rnd 2: [Knit to marker, p1 (1, 2, 2, 2, 2, 3, 3, 3, 3, 4, 4, 4, 4), work Chart A, p1 (1, 2, 2, 2, 2, 2, 3, 3, 3, 3, 4, 4, 4, 4), work Chart B, p1 (1, 2, 2, 2, 2, 2, 3, 3, 3, 3, 4, 4, 4, 4), work Chart C, p1 (1, 2, 2, 2, 2, 2, 3, 3, 3, 3, 4, 4, 4, 4)] twice.

Cont working body as est until pieces measures 7 (8, 8½, 9½, 10, 13, 15, 15½, 16, 17, 18, 18½, 19, 20, 20)" (or desired length to underarm) from CO ending with an even numbered rnd. It's a good idea to put all sts on waste yarn and block your sweater at this point to make sure it doesn't 'grow' too much with blocking.

Divide for Sleeves

Setup: K1 (3, 3, 6, 8, 10, 12, 4, 6, 10, 13, 11, 16, 20, 25) sts. This will now be the beg of the Row; place marker.

Row 1: K1 (3, 3, 6, 8, 10, 12, 4, 6, 10, 13, 11, 16, 20, 25) sts, p1 (1, 2, 2, 2, 2, 2, 3, 3, 3, 3, 4, 4, 4, 4) work Chart A, p1 (1, 2, 2, 2, 2, 2, 3, 3, 3, 3, 4, 4, 4, 4), work Chart B, p1 (1, 2, 2, 2, 2, 2, 3, 3, 3, 3, 4, 4, 4, 4), work Chart C, p1 (1, 2, 2, 2, 2, 2, 3, 3, 3, 3, 4, 4, 4, 4) k3 (5, 5, 8, 10, 12, 14, 8, 12, 17, 21, 19, 24, 28, 33), TURN, placing all other sts on hold for back. 48 (52, 56, 62, 66, 70, 74, 80, 84, 92, 98, 104, 114, 122, 132) sts. Cont working in pattern on these sts only until piece measures 1½ (2½, 3, 3½, 4, 4½, 4½, 4, 4½, 5, 5½, 6, 6½, 7, 7½)" from sleeve split, ending with a WS row.

Work dec row: [K12 (14, 16, 19, 21, 23, 25, 22, 24, 28, 31, 34, 39, 43, 48) [k2tog, k1] 8 (8, 8, 8, 8, 8, 8, 12, 12, 12, 12, 12, 12, 12, 12) times, k 12 (14, 16, 19, 21, 23, 25, 22, 23, 27, 31, 34, 39, 43, 48)] twice 40 (44, 48, 54, 58, 62, 66, 68, 72, 80, 86, 92, 102, 110, 120) sts.

Change to smaller needles and work in garter st, (knitting every row) for 2 (2, 2, 2, 2, 2, 2, 3, 3, 3, 3, 3, 3, 3, 3)". Place sts on hold.

Return back sts to larger needles and work back same as front.

Join shoulders:
Holding wrong sides of front and back tog join 5 (6, 8, 10, 12, 14, 15, 16, 17, 21, 24, 26, 29, 32, 38) sts at each shoulder edge using a 3-needle BO. BO all other sts.

Felicia Lo & SweetGeorgia Yarns

COLOUR, ART, DESIGN, AND TEXTILES HAVE PERVADED EVERY PART OF my life since I was a child. I was born and raised mainly in Vancouver, steps away from the beach where I spent many evenings watching the colours of the sky shift into night.

My obsession with textiles began very early on when I taught myself to knit and sew as a child, breaking my mother's sewing machine in the process. I always had a basket of yarn and needles by my bedside throughout high school and knit my first sweater during the summer before starting high school.

After finishing my degree in Pharmaceutical Sciences at University of British Columbia, I started a knitting blog in 2004, and a year later I founded SweetGeorgia Yarns with nothing but three skeins of hand-dyed sock yarn posted on Etsy.

Eight years later, SweetGeorgia is an artisan hand-dyed yarn company that is focused on making exquisite knitting yarns and spinning fibres in stunningly saturated colours. I can't imagine a more perfect life – living in Vancouver with my husband and surrounded by yarn and colour every day.

Sleeves

Starting at underarm and using larger needles, pick up 30 (32, 34, 36, 40, 44, 46, 52, 58, 60, 64, 70, 76, 82, 86) sts, pm, and join for working in the rnd. Work, knitting every rnd, until sleeve measures 3½ (4, 5, 6½, 7, 8, 9, 9, 7½, 7½, 8½, 7, 7, 6, 4½)" from pick up.

Dec rnd: K1, k2tog, knit to 3 sts before end of rnd, ssk, k1. 2 sts dec'd.

Knit 4 rnds. Rep these last 5 rnds until 28 (30, 32, 34, 36, 36, 38, 40, 40, 42, 46, 48, 50, 54, 54) sts rem.

Change to smaller needles and work in garter st for 2 (2, 2, 2, 2, 2, 2, 3, 3, 3, 3, 3, 3, 3, 3)". BO loosely. Rep for second sleeve.

Weave in your ends and block your finished sweater well.

CHART A
Repeat Rows 1–6.

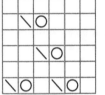

6
5
4
3
2
1

CHART C
Repeat Rows 1–6

6
5
4
3
2
1

CHART NOTES

From the cuff to underarm, garment is knit in rounds. When knit in rounds, all chart rounds are knit from right to left, and all chart sts are knit on all even-numbered rounds.

From underarm to shoulder, garment is knit in rows. When knitting in rows, RS (odd-numbered) rows are read from right to left, and WS (even-numbered) rows are read from left to right, and all chart sts are purled on all WS rows.

CHART B (CHILD SIZES)
Repeat Rows 3–10

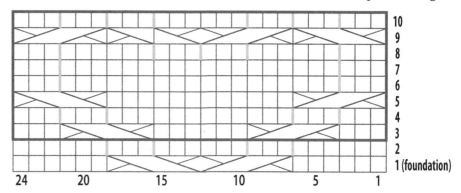

CHART B (ADULT SIZES)
Repeat Rows 5–12

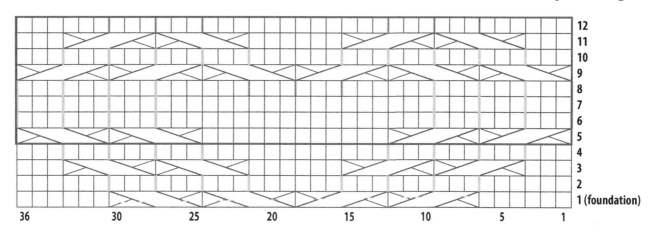

	k – knit on RS, purl on WS				path of cable
	yo – yarn over				pattern repeat
	ssk – slip, slip, knit			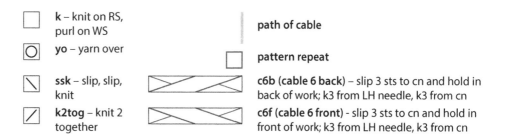	c6b (cable 6 back) – slip 3 sts to cn and hold in back of work; k3 from LH needle, k3 from cn
	k2tog – knit 2 together				c6f (cable 6 front) - slip 3 sts to cn and hold in front of work; k3 from LH needle, k3 from cn

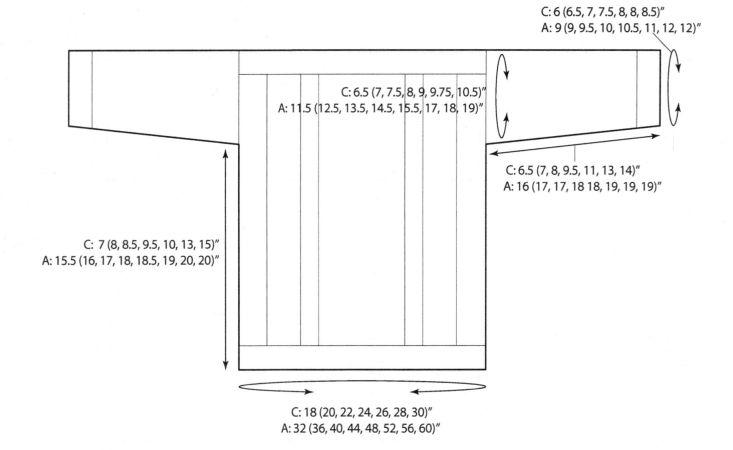

C: 6 (6.5, 7, 7.5, 8, 8, 8.5)"
A: 9 (9, 9.5, 10, 10.5, 11, 12, 12)"

C: 6.5 (7, 7.5, 8, 9, 9.75, 10.5)"
A: 11.5 (12.5, 13.5, 14.5, 15.5, 17, 18, 19)"

C: 6.5 (7, 8, 9.5, 11, 13, 14)"
A: 16 (17, 17, 18 18, 19, 19, 19)"

C: 7 (8, 8.5, 9.5, 10, 13, 15)"
A: 15.5 (16, 17, 18, 18.5, 19, 20, 20)"

C: 18 (20, 22, 24, 26, 28, 30)"
A: 32 (36, 40, 44, 48, 52, 56, 60)"

SCHEMATIC NOTE

In the schematic above, children's sizes are listed first
(labeled C:), and adult sizes are listed second (labeled A:).

Redcedar

Emily Wessel

R EDCEDAR IS A LACE STOLE FEATURING LARGE-SCALE BUT simple-to-work lace panels, arranged to resemble the book-matched wood boards of a rough-sawn floor. Worked in a rustic aran-weight yarn, the piece is big, bold, and oversized. Knit in a subtly variegated fingering-weight yarn, however, the piece is more delicate and refined.

REQUIRED SKILLS

Basic knitting skills; working lace from charted instruction

OPTIONS

Aran (fingering); Aran-weight version shown in brown; fingering-weight version shown in orange

FINISHED MEASUREMENTS

Length: 92 (84)" (or desired length)
Width: 20 (18)"

MATERIALS

Aran version

Cascade Ecological Wool (100% wool; 478 yds/437m per 250g skein); colour: 8087 Chocolate; 2 skeins)

About the Designer

Emily is co-founder and designer at Tin Can Knits, where she designs exquisite patterns for hand-knitting and crafts in-depth tutorials. Born and raised on Vancouver Island, Canada, she now works, knits, and enjoys sweater weather in the beautiful city of Edinburgh, UK.

US #9/5.5mm needles, or size needed to obtain gauge

Fingering version

Everything Old Kashmir Sock (80% merino wool, 10% nylon, 10% cashmere; 435 yds/398m per 100g skein); colour: Havana Club; 3 skeins

US #6/4mm needles, or size needed to obtain gauge

Both versions

4-6 stitch markers
Yarn needle
Blocking wires and pins

GAUGE

Measured over one lace panel, after blocking: 19 sts wide × 42 rows long

Aran weight: panel measures 6½" wide × 7½" long

Fingering weight: 4½" wide × 6" long

Gauge is not critical in this pattern, but a different gauge will affect yardage required and size of finished item.

PATTERN

CO 63 (82) sts. Knit 7 (9) rows.

Establish Lace Pattern

Note: You may wish to place markers to indicate the beg and end of lace panels.

Aran version:
Row 1 (RS): P4, work Panel A over next 19 sts, work Panel B over next 19 sts, work Panel A over next 19 sts, p2.
Row 2 (WS): Purl.

Fingering version:
Row 1 (RS): P4, [work Panel A over next 19 sts, work Panel B over next 19 sts] twice, p2.
Row 2 (WS): Purl.

Both versions: Cont in pattern as est, following Chart A and repeating rows 1–42 of lace pattern until desired length of scarf or stole is reached, or you are close to the end of the yarn.

Knit 8 (10) rows. BO all sts loosely.

Finishing

Weave in all yarn ends then wet block finished piece aggressively to open up and set the lace pattern.

Emma Galati & Everything Old

I AM A BORN-AND-RAISED VANCOUVER ISLANDER, and I am very lucky to have spent my childhood exploring the lovely islands and oceans of the west coast on the family sailboat.

I moved to Scotland at 18 and then spent a few busy years in Toronto before coming to my senses and realizing the best place in the world is right here on the coast. I spent a few years working toward a degree in fashion design at Ryerson University before realizing the industry wasn't for me, and then completed my BA in my great academic love, art history, here in Victoria.

I was married in 2007 and began knitting in 2008 as a way to save money (HA!) on gifts for my numerous in-laws. Before long I was dyeing, spinning, designing, and weaving. I brought my passions for fashion, textiles, design, art, and colour together when I began dyeing yarn for Everything Old in spring 2011. Working with yarn and fibre and owning my small business has been immensely rewarding. When I'm not elbow-deep in pots of soggy yarn, I am a stay-at-home parent to my three-year-old daughter.

CHART A
Wood Grain Lace; repeat Rows 1-42

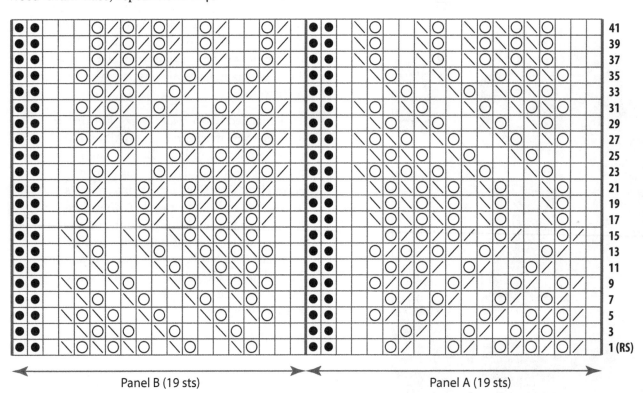

Panel B (19 sts)   Panel A (19 sts)

CHART NOTES

- Chart shows RS (odd-numbered rows only.
- All WS rows: Purl all sts.
- Work Panels A & B as described in pattern text.

☐ **k** – knit

● **p** – purl

O **yo** – yarn over

\ **ssk** – slip, slip, knit

/ **k2tog** – knit 2 together

☐ **pattern repeat**

Sea Wall

Alexa Ludeman

THESE SOCKS ARE KNIT FROM CUFF TO TOE. The cables mimic the mighty Lions Gate bridge, which is visible whilst you stroll along the Stanley Park Sea Wall in Vancouver, a very popular spot for locals and tourists alike.

About the Designer

Alexa has been designing knitwear for a few years now, most recently as part of the design duo Tin Can Knits. She loves it all, from simple textures to lace and cables and everything in between! She finds design inspiration from the natural wonders of her home in the Pacific Northwest.

REQUIRED SKILLS

Basic knitting skills; knitting in the round; knitting with double pointed needles or magic loop; increases/decreases; short rows; kitchener stitch; working simple cables from chart; twisted stitches; slipped stitches; picking up stitches

SIZES

Women's S (M, L); shown in size M

FINISHED MEASUREMENTS

Foot circumference: 7½ (8, 8½)"

Foot and leg length are adjustable.

MATERIALS

Sweet Fiber Yarns Cashmerino Sock (80% superwash merino, 10% cashmere, 10% nylon, 340 m per 115 gm skein); sample uses colour Tea Leaves. Substitute 350 (370, 400) yds sock-weight yarn.

US #1/2.25mm and US #2/2.75mm needles for working in the round: dpns, 1 long circular or 2 short circulars

Cable needle

GAUGE

28 sts and 40 rnds = 4"/10cm in St st on larger needles

48 sts and 40 rnds = 4"/10cm in twisted rib unstretched on smaller needles

Cable Chart measures 2½".

STITCHES AND TECHNIQUES

M1P (make 1 purlwise): Insert left needle, from front to back, under the horizontal strand which lies between the st just knit, and the following st; then purl into the back of this lp. 1 st inc'd.

K1tbl: knit 1 st through the back lp.

P1tbl: purl 1 st through the back lp.

PATTERN

Leg

Using smaller needles, CO 60 (64, 68) sts. Distribute sts across needles as you prefer and join for working in the rnd.

Ribbing rnd: (K1tbl [see Stitches and Techniques], p1) around. Work in ribbing as est until piece measures 2" from cast-on edge.

Change to larger needles.

Pattern setup rnd: [K1tbl, p1] 3 (4, 5) times, k2, p4, k4, p4, k2, m1p (see Stitches and Techniques), (k1tbl, p1) to end. 61 (65, 69) sts.

Rnd 1: [k1tbl, p1] 3 (4, 5) times, work chart across next 16 sts, p1, (k1tbl, p1) to end. Cont in pattern as set until leg measures 6 (7, 7½)" from CO (or longer if desired).

Heel Flap

Turn so that WS is facing.

Set-up Row (RS): [K1tbl, p1] 3 (4, 5) times, work chart as set across next 16 sts, p1, (k1tbl, p1) 3 (4, 5) times, (this is the top of the foot), [k1tbl, p1] to end TURN. You will now be working only on the last 32 sts).

Row 1 (WS): Sl 1, p1tbl (see Stitches and Techniques), [k1, p1tbl] 15 times. The heel will be worked only on these 32 sts.

Row 2 (RS): Sl 1, p1, [k1tbl, p1] 15 times.

Row 3 (WS): Sl 1, p1tbl, [k1, p1tbl] 15 times. Rep Rows 2 & 3 a total of 15 more times. 33 heel rows total.

Heel Turn

Row 1 (RS): Sl 1, k 17, ssk, k1, turn.
Row 2 (WS): Sl 1, p5, p2tog, p1, turn.

Row 3 (RS): Sl 1, knit to 1 st before the gap, ssk, k1, turn.
Row 4 (WS): Sl 1, purl to 1 st before the gap, p2tog, p1, turn. Rep Rows 3 & 4 until you have 1 st rem after you turn.

Next Row: Sl 1, knit to last 2 sts, ssk, turn.
Next Row: Sl 1, purl to last 2 sts, p2tog, turn. 18 heel sts rem.

Gusset and Foot

Knit rem heel sts. With RS facing, pick up and knit 17 sts along first side of heel flap; work across 29 (33, 37) instep sts in pattern as set; pick up and knit 17 sts along heel flap and knit across 8 (9, 9) heel sts. 81 (85, 89) sts total. This is the new start of rnd. Rearrange sts and place marker as required.

Rnd 1: Knit to 3 sts before start of instep, k2tog, k1; work across instep sts in pattern as set; k1, ssk, knit to end of rnd.

Rnd 2: Knit to instep; work across instep sts in pattern as set; knit to end of rnd. Rep Rnds 1 & 2 another 9 times until you have a total of 61 (65, 69) sts.

Rep rnd 2 until foot reaches 6½ (7, 7½)" from heel (or 1½" short of desired length).

Toe

Size S only:
Set-up Rnd 1: Knit to end of instep, k1, ssk, knit to 3 sts before end of rnd, k2tog, k1. 59 sts.

Set-up Rnd 2: K1, ssk, knit to end of instep, k1, ssk, knit to 3 sts before end of rnd, k2tog, k1. 56 sts.

Size M only:
Set-up Rnd 1: K1, ssk, knit to end. 64 sts.

Size L only:
Set-up Rnd 1: K1, ssk, knit to 3 sts before end of instep, k2tog, k1, knit to end. 2 sts dec'd.
Work Set-up Rnd 1 once more. 65 sts.
Set-up Rnd 2: K1, ssk, knit to end. 64 sts.

All sizes:
Rnd 1: Knit.
Rnd 2: K1, ssk, knit to 3 sts before end of instep, k2tog, k1; k1, ssk, knit to 3 sts before end of rnd, k2tog, k1. Rep Rnds 1 & 2 until 48 sts rem.

Rep Rnd 2 until 24 sts rem.
Using Kitchener st, graft toe closed.

Finishing

Block and weave in ends; wear proudly on your sea-wall stroll!

☐	**k** – knit
⊡	**p** – purl
	path of cable
☐	**pattern repeat**

2/2 RC – Sl next 2 sts onto cn and hold in front of work; k2, k2 from cn.
2/2 LC – Sl next 2 sts onto cn and hold in back of work; k2, k2 from cn.
2/1 RCp – Sl next st onto cn and hold in back of work, k2, p1 from cn.
2/1 LCp – Sl next 2 sts onto cn and hold in front of work, p1, k2 from cn.

CHART NOTES
- Chart shows all rounds. Read chart from right to left.
- Refer to text instructions for chart placement.

SEA WALL CHART

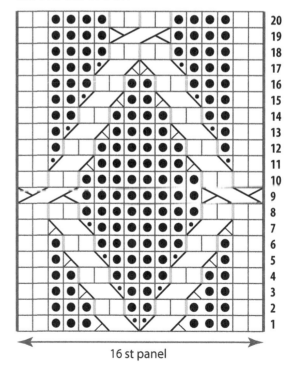

16 st panel

Meet Megan Goodacre

WE FIRST MET MEGAN WHEN SHE GRACIOUSLY SENT US HER CUSTOM TRICKSY Knitter's notebooks as giveaways for our second Knit Social retreat, Yarn Camp. They were a huge hit! We knew her designs from Ravelry already, but were surprised to learn that she lived in Courtenay, BC. Her quietly elegant aesthetic is so clean yet pretty, that we really should have known she was a Coastal BC'er. Her pullover design for Cascadia truly embodies the classic feminine style we admire her for. Knit in SweetGeorgia Worsted, it's a perfect weekend sweater, but Megan also suggested a linen yarn which we think would be stunning.

—*Amanda and Fiona*

Amanda & Fiona: *Where were you born? How long have you lived in BC? What brought you here if you weren't born or raised here?*

Megan: Although I'm living in Ottawa now, and have lived in Victoria, Vancouver, Courtenay, and France, I was born in Victoria, and will always think of that as home.

What is the most inspiring part of BC for you?

The variety of scale and climate, from the tiniest tide pool at Botanical Beach to the immense slopes of the Rockies. The quality of the light, always filtered by woods and water. The mildness of the seasons. It always strikes me as a calm and reasonable place to live.

Who taught you to knit?

My mom, when I was six.

What was the catalyst that took you from knitting to design? What did you do prior to this or what do you in addition to this as an occupation?

Professionally, I've tended towards left-brained occupations. My bread-winning career, until recently, has been programming and graphic design. I've sewn and knit for decades, and have once or twice tried sewing as a profession, but have been discouraged by the increasing under-valuing of handcrafts.

But in recent years, the shift in communication via the web and groups like Ravelry, combined with a revived interest in textiles, craft, and DIY, has transformed the landscape for the creative professional. Designing knitting projects, writing patterns, constructing schematics, grading sizes, marketing on the web, and teaching others, has turned out to be the ideal blend for me.

What is your favorite part of your job?

I really enjoy the enthusiasm and generosity of test knitters; it changes the process from a solitary activity to a group project.

Tell us about your design process.

I'm always looking for balance. Getting just the right amount of visual detail but keeping the pattern simple. Leaving room for the knitter to adjust the pattern but including each and every step. It's a constant learning process for me, where I revisit and simplify the sketch and schematic several times before writing the pattern. I usually write the pattern in full before starting; it forces me to go through the mental exercise of solving problems in a virtual sense instead of on the needles.

What's the most unreasonable request you've made of your spouse/partner/ companion to enable your knitting?

To allow me to turn the dining room table into a light table for several weeks.

Where is the strangest place you've ever knit?

I'm pretty conservative. Does a movie theatre qualify as strange? I do occasionally knit while driving, but only at really long red lights.

Courtenay

Megan Goodacre

THIS RELAXED, LONG-SLEEVE PULLOVER, KNIT IN worsted-weight yarn, is perfect for wearing while gazing at misty morning tide pools or taking quiet walks in the forest. Inspired by the thick woods and windy bluffs of Vancouver Island's coastline, Courtenay is a flattering and comfortable sweater, with carefully placed and understated details. Simple eyelets at the neck, pockets, and cuffs add texture, while short-row shaping at the back neck and lower edge make for a lovely fit. You'll enjoy the top-down seamless construction, hybrid circular/raglan yoke, and knit-in pockets. Rugged but feminine, Courtenay is a quick and versatile knit.

About the Designer

Megan Goodacre is a knitter and graphic artist who strives for simplicity and elegance in her designs. Recently transplanted from Canada's Vancouver Island to its snowy capital, Ottawa, Megan can often be found huddled next to her computer for warmth, working on her website, TricksyKnitter.com.

REQUIRED SKILLS

Basic knitting skills; knitting in the round; increases/decreases; backward loop cast on; cable cast on; short rows; knowledge of basic sweater construction; picking up stitches; seaming

SIZES

Women's XS (S, M, L, XL, 2X, 3X); shown in size S

Intended to be worn with 2–4" of positive ease.

FINISHED MEASUREMENTS

Bust: 33 (37½, 40¾, 45¼, 49½, 53)"

Length: 24 (25, 25½, 26¼, 26¾, 27½)"

MATERIALS

SweetGeorgia Yarns Superwash Worsted (100% superwash merino wool; 200 yds/183m per 115g skein); color: Cypress; 5 (6, 6, 7, 8, 8) skeins

24- or 29-inch circular needles, plus needle(s) for your preferred method of working in a small round for the neck and sleeves, in the following sizes:

- US #8/5mm
- US #7/4.5mm, or sizes needed to obtain gauge

6 ring stitch markers (1 of these in a contrast color)
Yarn needle
Stitch holders or waste yarn
2 spare dpns for marking pocket position

GAUGE

18½ sts and 24 rnds = 4"/10cm in St st, blocked, on larger needles

PATTERN NOTES

Courtenay is worked in the round from the top down. After the seed-stitch neck band, short rows raise the back neck.

The wraps from the short rows are hidden by the purl stitches of the seed stitch pattern and do not need to be picked up later. The front upper yoke uses circular yoke shaping with yarnovers.

Pockets are knit in. The body's lower edge is shaped with short rows. Again, the wraps are placed to be concealed by the purls of the seed-stitch edge.

The sleeve's underarm is picked up from the body's underarm, and the sleeve is worked in the round with eyelet details at the cuff.

STITCHES AND TECHNIQUES

Seed stitch (over a multiple of 2 sts, worked in the rnd)
Rnd 1: [P1, k1] to end.
Rnd 2: [K1, p1].
Rep Rnds 1 & 2 for patt.

PATTERN

Neck

With smaller needles for working in a small rnd, CO 92 (96, 96, 100, 100, 104) sts. Being careful not to twist sts, join for working in the rnd. Place marker for start of rnd. The start of rnd is at the left back shoulder.

Work 2 rnds seed stitch (see Stitches and Techniques).

Next rnd: Cont in seed stitch, placing 4 markers as foll: work 28 (30, 32, 34, 36, 38) (back), pm, 15 (15, 13, 13, 11, 11) (right sleeve), pm, 34 (36, 38, 40, 42, 44) (front), pm, 15 (15, 13, 13, 11, 11) (left sleeve).

Back neck short rows:
Switch to larger needles.
Note: there is no need to pick up and hide the wraps – they are concealed nicely in the seed stitch.

Short Row 1 (RS) (Inc): K1, m1L, knit to 1 st before marker, m1R, k1, sm, k1, m1L, k1, w&t. 2 sts inc'd in back, 1 st inc'd in right sleeve. 30 (32, 34, 36, 38, 40) sts for back, 16 (16, 14, 14, 12, 12) sts for right sleeve. (Note that all wraps should be around a st that is a purl on the RS.)

Short Row 2 (WS): Purl to 3 sts past start of rnd marker, w&t.

Short Row 3 (Inc): [Knit to 1 st before marker, m1R, k1, sm, k1, m1L] twice, k6, w&t. 2 sts inc'd in back, 1 st inc'd in each sleeve. 32 (34, 36, 38, 40, 42) sts for back, 17 (17, 15, 15, 13, 13) sts for right sleeve, 16 (16, 14, 14, 12, 12) sts for left sleeve.

Short Row 4: Purl to 8 sts past start of rnd marker, w&t.

Short Row 5 (Inc): [Knit to 1 st before marker, m1R, k1, sm, k1, m1L] twice, k11, w&t. 2 sts inc'd in back, 1 st inc'd in each sleeve. 34 (36, 38, 40, 42, 44) back, 18 (18, 16, 16, 14, 14) right sleeve, 17 (17, 15, 15, 13, 13) left sleeve.

Short Row 6: Purl to 13 sts past start of rnd marker, w&t.

Short Row 7 (Inc): Knit to 1 st before marker, m1R, k1. 1 st inc'd in left sleeve. 18 (18, 16, 16, 14, 14) left sleeve.

Knit 1 rnd even.

Upper Yoke

The upper yoke combines raglan increases on the back and sleeves with yarnover increases across the front.

Rnd 1 (¾ Raglan Inc): [K1, m1L, knit to 1 st before marker, m1R, k1, sm] twice, knit across front to marker, sm, then rep between [ ] once more. 2 sts inc'd in back, 2 sts inc'd in each sleeve. 36 (38, 40, 42, 44, 46) back, 20 (20, 18, 18, 16, 16) each sleeve.

Rnd 2 and all even rnds: Knit.

Rnd 3 (¾ Raglan Inc): Rep Rnd 1. 2 sts inc'd in back, 2 sts inc'd in each sleeve. 38 (40, 42, 44, 46, 48) back, 22 (22, 20, 20, 18, 18) each sleeve.

Rnd 5 (¾ Raglan + Front Yarnover Inc): [K1, m1L, knit to 1 st before marker, m1R, k1, sm] twice, k2 (3, 4, 5, 6, 7), (yo, k6) 5 times, yo, k2 (3, 4, 5, 6, 7) to marker, sm, then rep between [ ] once more. 2 sts inc'd in back, 6 sts inc'd in front, 2 sts inc'd in each sleeve. 40 (42, 44, 46, 48, 50) back, 40 (42, 44, 46, 48, 50) front, 24 (24, 22, 22, 20, 20) each sleeve.

Rnd 7 (¾ Raglan Inc): Rep Rnd 1. 2 sts inc'd in back, 2 sts inc'd in each sleeve. 42 (44, 46, 48, 50, 52) back, 26 (26, 24, 24, 22, 22) each sleeve.

Rnd 9 (¾ Raglan + Front Yarnover Inc): [K1, m1L, knit to 1 st before marker, m1R, k1, sm] twice, k6 (7, 8, 9, 10, 11), (yo, k7) 4 times, yo, k6 (7, 8, 9, 10, 11) to marker, sm, then rep between [ ] once more. 2 sts inc'd in back, 5 sts inc'd in front, 2 sts inc'd in each sleeve. 44 (46, 48, 50, 52, 54) back, 45 (47, 49, 51, 53, 55) front, 28 (28, 26, 26, 24, 24) each sleeve.

Rnd 11 (¾ Raglan Inc): Rep Rnd 1. 2 sts inc'd in back, 2 sts inc'd in each sleeve. 46 (48, 50, 52, 54, 56) back, 30 (30, 28, 28, 26, 26) each sleeve.

Rnd 13 (¾ Raglan + Front Yarnover Inc): [K1, m1L, knit to 1 st before marker, m1R, k1, sm] twice, k2 (3, 4, 5, 6, 7), (yo, k8) 5 times, yo, k3 (4, 5, 6, 7, 8) to marker, sm, then rep between [ ] once more. 2 sts inc'd in back, 6 sts inc'd in front, 2 sts inc'd in each sleeve. 48 (50, 52, 54, 56, 58) back, 51 (53, 55, 57, 59, 61) front, 32 (32, 30, 30, 28, 28) each sleeve.

Rnd 15 (¾ Raglan Inc): Rep Rnd 1. 2 sts inc'd in back, 2 sts inc'd in each sleeve. 50 (52, 54, 56, 58, 60) back, 34 (34, 32, 32, 30, 30) each sleeve.

Rnd 16: Knit.

Lower Yoke

Read ahead before proceeding with this section!

Body Only Inc rnds will be worked as foll: [K1, m1L, knit to 1 st before marker, m1R, k1, sm, knit to marker, sm] twice. 2 sts inc'd in each front and back.

Full Raglan Inc rnds will be worked as foll: [K1, m1L, knit to 1 st before marker, m1R, k1, sm] 4 times. 2 sts inc'd in each front and back, 2 sts inc'd in each sleeve.

Knit all rnds, working increases every other rnd using the foll schedule:

Alternate Body Only and Full Raglan Inc rnds 0 (1, 1, 3, 4, 4) times. 50 (56, 58, 68, 74, 76) back, 51 (57, 59, 69, 75, 77) front, 34 (36, 34, 38, 38, 38) each sleeve.

Work Full Raglan Inc rnds 10 (10, 11, 10, 11, 13) times. 70 (76, 80, 88, 96, 102) back, 71 (77, 81, 89, 97, 103) front, 54 (56, 56, 58, 60, 64) each sleeve.

Knit 1 rnd.

Separate Sleeves, Work Body

Work across back to first marker, transfer right sleeve sts to scrap yarn, removing markers on either side of sleeve. Using backward lp method, CO 3 (5, 7, 8, 9, 10), place marker for side, CO 3 (5, 7, 8, 9, 10). Work across front to next sleeve, set aside second sleeve and CO second underarm same as first, placing marker for left side of body and new beg of rnd. 153 (173, 189, 209, 229, 245) sts.

Knit 17 rnds.

Next rnd (Dec): [K1, k2tog, work to 3 sts before next marker, ssk, k1, sm] twice. 4 sts dec'd.

Knit 17 rnds.

Work 1 more Dec rnd. 145 (165, 181, 201, 221, 237) sts. Cont knitting even, until the sweater measures 8" from underarms.

Please read Inc and Pocket instructions before continuing.

Next rnd (Inc): [K1, m1L, knit to 1 st before marker, m1R, k1] twice. 4 sts inc'd. Cont even. When body measures 10 (10¼, 10¼, 10½, 10½, 10¾)" from underarm, begin pockets as below, AT THE SAME TIME, work 2 more Inc rnds every 14th rnd. 8 sts inc'd, 157 (177, 193, 213, 233, 249) sts.

Pockets

(If the beg of pocket coincides with Inc rnd, save Inc for following rnd.)

Setup rnd: Knit across back to marker; k2 (4, 6, 8, 10, 12) sts, slip next 23 (25, 25, 25, 27, 27) sts to holder, pm, CO 23 (25, 25, 25, 27, 27) sts using backward loop, knit to 25 (29, 31, 33, 37, 39) before end of rnd, slip next 23 (25, 25, 25, 27, 27) sts to holder, pm, CO 23 (25, 25, 25, 27, 27) sts, pm, work to end.

Next 3 rnds: [Knit to pocket marker; work seed stitch to next marker] twice, knit to end of rnd.

Knit 3 rnds.

Eyelet rnd: [Knit to pocket marker; K2 (3, 3, 3, 4, 4), [yo, k2tog, k4] 3 times, yo, k2tog, k1 (2, 2, 2, 3, 3)] twice, knit to end of rnd.

Once side shaping and pockets are complete, remove pocket markers and knit even until body measures 14¼ (14½, 14½, 14½, 14¾, 14¾)" from underarms.

Shape Bottom Edge

Next rnd (Dec): Knit to marker, sm, [k18 (20, 22, 25, 27, 29), k2tog] 3 times, k19 (23, 25, 26, 30, 32) to marker. 3 sts dec'd, 154 (174, 190, 210, 230, 246) sts.

Note: there is no need to hide the wraps as you work through this, the wraps should be concealed by the purls.

Short Row 1: Knit to 4 sts before marker, w&t.
Short Row 2: Purl to 5 sts before marker, w&t.
Short Row 3: Knit to 8 sts before marker, w&t.
Short Row 4: Purl to 9 sts before marker, w&t.
Short Row 5: Knit to 18 sts before marker, w&t.
Short Row 6: Purl to 19 sts before marker, w&t.

Place marker (this is start of rnd for the next 8 rnds). Switch to smaller needles. Work 8 rnds seed stitch, starting with a knit st. Bind off.

Sleeves

Work both the same.
Transfer sleeve sts to larger needles for working in a small rnd. Join yarn and starting at center of underarm, pick up and knit 3 (5, 7,

8, 9, 10) sts, knit across sleeve, pick up and knit 3 (5, 7, 8, 9, 10) sts, pm for beg of rnd. 60 (66, 70, 74, 78, 84) sts.

Knit 12 (9, 8, 7, 7, 7) rnds.

Next rnd (Dec): K1, k2tog, knit to 3 sts before end of rnd, ssk, k1. 2 sts dec'd. Cont knitting, working a Dec rnd every 11 (9, 8, 8, 7, 6)th rnd 5 (6, 7, 7, 9, 11) more times. 10 (12, 14, 14, 18, 22) dec'd, 48 (52, 54, 58, 58, 60) sts.

Knit 4 rnds.

Next rnd (Eyelet inc): K18 (20, 21, 23, 23, 24), [yo, k4] 3 times, yo, k18 (20, 21, 23, 23, 24). 4 sts inc'd, 52 (56, 58, 62, 62, 64) sts.

Knit 3 rnds.

Next rnd (Eyelet inc): K16 (18, 19, 21, 21, 22), [yo, k5] 4 times, yo, k16 (18, 19, 21, 21, 22). 5 sts inc'd, 57 (61, 63, 67, 67, 69) sts.

Knit until sleeve measures 17¼ (17½, 17½, 18, 18¼, 18¾)" from underarm.

Next rnd (Dec): K0 (1, 2, 0, 0, 0), [K4 (3, 3, 3, 3, 3), k2tog] 9 (11, 11, 13 13, 13) times, knit to end. 48 (50, 52, 54, 54, 56) sts.

Switch to smaller needles. Work 8 rnds seed stitch. Bind off.

Pocket Linings

Work both the same.
Transfer held pocket sts to larger needles. Work in St st until pocket lining reaches top of seed stitch. Bind off.

Finishing

Block.

Pocket linings: With spare dpns, mark position to stitch pocket on WS of body. Whip stitch linings in place. If necessary, use duplicate stitch to tighten sts at edge of pocket openings.

Weave in ends. At the same time, use duplicate stitch to tighten any loose sts at underarms.

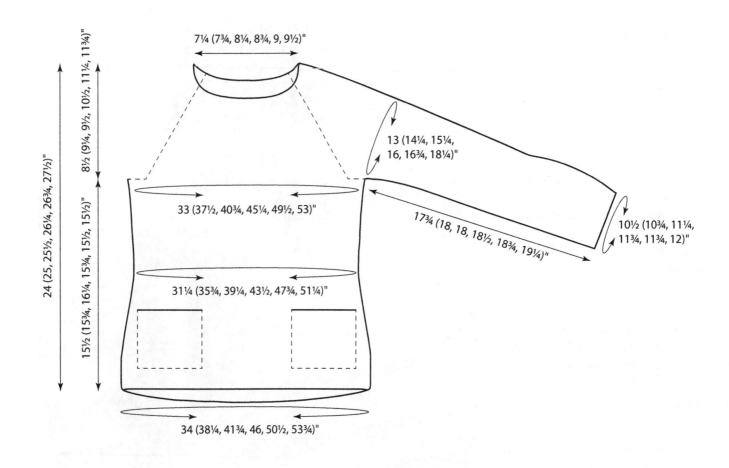

7¼ (7¾, 8¼, 8¾, 9, 9½)"

13 (14¼, 15¼, 16, 16¾, 18¼)"

33 (37½, 40¾, 45¼, 49½, 53)"

17¾ (18, 18, 18½, 18¾, 19¼)"

10½ (10¾, 11¼, 11¾, 11¾, 12)"

31¼ (35¾, 39¼, 43½, 47¾, 51¼)"

24 (25, 25½, 26¼, 26¾, 27½)"

8½ (9¼, 9½, 10½, 11¼, 11¾)"

15½ (15¾, 16¼, 15¾, 15½, 15½)"

34 (38¼, 41¾, 46, 50½, 53¾)"

Meet Judy Marples

JUDY IS ANOTHER DESIGNER WHOSE PATTERNS WE KNEW BEFORE WE HAD THE pleasure of meeting her. Her gorgeous lace shawls have been filling up my queue for a couple of years now, and she keeps writing patterns faster than I can knit them! Judy works at one of our very favourite yarn shops, 88 Stitches in Langley, BC, and is just simply a lovely person. Raven's Nest was the very first design submission that we received for *Cascadia*, and as soon as we saw it we knew that it would be in the book, no question about it. —*Amanda*

Where were you born? How long have you lived in BC?

I was born and raised in the suburbs of Vancouver and have lived on the West Coast most of my life.

What was the catalyst that took you from knitting to design? What did you do prior to this or what do you in addition to this as an occupation?

I was in banking for years before joining the fibre world full time. I began by working in yarn shops and shortly after that I started teaching knitting classes. I decided to try designing on a whim just to see if I could do it. I fell in love with the whole process! I still work part time in my LYS and teach classes, and in between I work on my designs.

Most useful knitting/crafting tip?

If things are not going well, give the project a time out. Some space away from it will give you a fresh perspective and that will usually solve all problems.

Tell us about your most epic knitting disaster.

There have been several but there was a cabled cardigan I knit way back when I was inexperienced and didn't know the importance of gauge. I cast on with the recommended needle size and yarn and knit the whole sweater without stopping to measure the size. I didn't know it at the time, but I am a loose knitter and always have to use a smaller size needle to get gauge.

Of course, the sweater turned out fine in length but absolutely massive in width. I was crushed after doing all that work and too heartbroken to rip it out and start over.

My sister saved the day though. When I showed her the sweater, she sized it up and decided that she could fix it using her newly acquired Serger. We pinned in the side seams and she serged off at least 6 inches at the seams and it fit fairly well! I wore that sweater for years and years.

Tell us about the project you're most proud of.

I think that would be my design Dover Castle Shawl. It was my first "for sale" pattern. I worked really hard on the design, coming up with the original stitch pattern, and it was so well received that I was thrilled. It made me realize that design work was what I wanted to do.

What's the most unreasonable request you have made of your spouse/partner/ companion to enable your knitting?

My husband has cheerfully modeled lace shawls, hung knitwear from trees, and patiently waited while I browsed in a new yarn shop, usually while we have been on holiday. He regularly helps me edit and compare lace charts to written instruction. Fortunately for me, he thinks all of it is perfectly reasonable.

Where is the strangest place you've ever knit?

In a hotel bathroom! I was sharing a hotel room with my sister-in-law and I couldn't sleep. This particular room had only one light, a huge one, in the ceiling. I knew I would wake her up if I turned it on so I quietly gathered up my knitting in the dark and went into the bathroom and shut the door. I put the lid down on the toilet and sat down and knit for quite a while.

All went well until my sister-in-law woke up, stumbled into the bathroom and stopped short when she saw me sitting on the toilet knitting. The next morning she woke up and told me she had had the strangest dream!

Raven's Nest

Judy Marples

Raven's Nest was inspired by the landscapes and mythology of the beautiful west coast of Canada. The Raven is a First Nation's symbol of creation, knowledge, nature, and truth in all things. The Raven is a healer and a keeper of secrets. Raven's Nest is a triangular shawl featuring top-down construction and is easily adjustable to any size.

REQUIRED SKILLS

Basic knitting skills; increases/decreases; right and left increase; backward loop cast on; knitted cast on; garter tab cast on; Estonian bind off; working simple cables from chart or written instructions; working simple lace from chart or written instructions

FINISHED MEASUREMENTS

60" wide × 20" deep, after blocking

MATERIALS

Sweet Fiber Cashmerino Sock (80% merino, 10% cashmere, 10% nylon; 372 yds/340m per 115g skein); color: Nocturelle; 2 skeins (approx 488 yds/450m used for sample shown)

32-inch US#5/3.75mm circular needle, or size needed to obtain gauge

Removable stitch markers
Cable needle
Yarn needle

GAUGE

18 sts and 26 rows = 4"/10 cm in St st, after blocking

Gauge is not critical in this pattern, but a different gauge will affect yardage required and size of finished item.

PATTERN NOTES

The shawl begins at the centre top and is worked downward, finishing at the lower edge.

The shawl is made up of two sides separated by the centre spine st. The centre spine st is not shown on the chart and is worked in St st throughout. The 4 edge sts (2 sts at each end of every row) are not shown on the chart. The 4 edge stitches are worked in garter stitch (knit every row) throughout the pattern.

STITCHES AND TECHNIQUES

RLI (Right Lifted Increase): Insert the right needle into the st below the next st on the left needle. Pick up this st and place it on the left needle, then knit into it. 1 st inc'd.

LLI (Left Lifted Increase): Use the left needle to pick up the st 2 rows below the last stitch on the right needle. Knit into this st. 1 st inc'd.

3/2 RPC: Sl next 3 st to cn, hold in back. K2; sl p st from cn and p1; k2 from cn.

2/3 LPC: Sl next 3 sts to cn, hold in front. K2; sl p st from cn and p1; k2 from cn.

Estonian Bind Off: K1, *k1, slip these 2 sts back to the left needle and K2tog tbl. Cont, repeating from * until only 1 st rems. Cut yarn and pull through final st to secure.

PATTERN

CO 2 sts using the backward loop method.
Knit 6 rows.

Next row: K2, do not turn, rotate your work one quarter turn to the right and pick up and knit 3 sts along the left side edge of the garter ridges (one st for each garter ridge).

Turn the work another quarter turn to the right and pick up and knit two sts (the two backward lps) from the CO edge. 7 sts.
Next row (WS): K2, p1, pm, p1, pm, p1, k2.

You now have a marker on either side of the centre spine st. As you inc on either side of this st be sure to keep your markers next to this centre spine st.

Stockinette Stitch Section

Row 1 (RS): K2, yo, knit to the first marker, RLI (see Stitches and Techniques), sm, knit centre spine st, sm, LLI (see Stitches and Techniques), knit to last 2 sts, yo, k2. 4 sts inc'd.
Row 2 (WS): K2, purl to last 2 sts, k2.
Rep the above 2 rows until you have 183 sts.
Note: You may adjust the size of your St st section for a larger or smaller shawl by adjusting the total st count by multiples of 28 sts. For example, you may choose to knit this section to a total st count of

127, 155, 183, 211, 239 and so on. Altering the size of this section will also affect the yardage required for the shawl.

Lace Section

Work Rows 1–18 of the chart; 219 sts.

Work Rows 5–18 twice more, and then 5–10 again, adding in repeats of the pattern as required. 287 sts.

Final row (RS): K2, yo, knit to the first marker, RLI, sm, knit centre spine st, sm, LLI, knit to last 2 sts, yo, k2. 4 sts inc'd. 291 sts.

Bind Off

BO on the WS as foll:
Section A: CO 3 sts using a knitted CO. BO 3 sts tightly using the standard BO. Sl 1 pwise, pass first st on right needle over sl st and off needle. Pull on working yarn to tighten. Use the Estonian BO (see Stitches and Techniques) to BO 8 sts (the st already on the right needle counts as the first st of the BO).

Section B: *Pass st on right needle back to left needle, CO 3 sts using the knitted CO. BO 3 sts tightly using the standard BO. Sl 1 pwise, pass first st on right needle over sl st and off needle. Pull working yarn to tighten. BO 6 sts using the Estonian BO. Every second picot should be completed in the one st before each marker. Rep from * until 10 sts rem before the spine st. Rep Section A twice over the sts at the tip of the shawl. Rep Section B until there are 12 sts left on the needle. Rep Section A once (3 sts rem).

Use the Estonian bind off to BO an additional 2 sts. (1 st rem.)

Move st to left needle. CO 3 sts using the knitted CO. BO all sts tightly using the standard BO.

Cut the yarn and use the tail of yarn and a yarn needle to secure the last picot in place.

Finishing

Block as desired. I like to place blocking wires along the top edge first and secure with T-pins. Then place a blocking wire up the centre spine and pin on either side of this wire to secure. Finally pin out the bottom edge. Weave in ends.

About the Designer

Judy was born and raised and still happily lives on the beautiful west coast of Canada. Her favourite place to knit is on the ferry heading to Vancouver Island from the mainland. She loves all the little details that come together to form a design and always strives to create patterns that are intuitive for the knitter and fun to knit.

Find her on Ravelry as spinnyknitter and at her blog purlbumps.wordpress.com

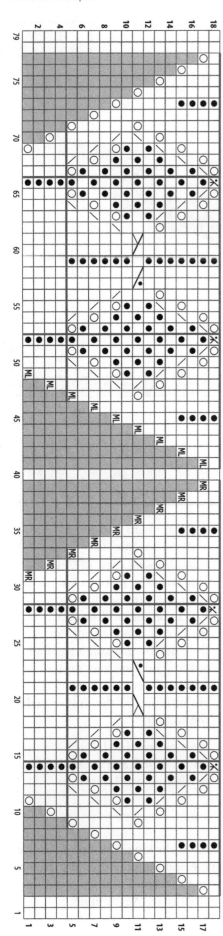

RAVEN'S NEST CHART

☐	k – knit	
●	p – purl	
○	yo – yarn over	
╲	ssk – slip, slip, knit	
╱	k2tog – knit 2 together	
☐	pattern repeat	
⊠	p3tog – purl 3 together	
ML	LLI – left lifted inc	
MR	RLI – right lifted inc	

3/2 RPC – Sl next 3 st to cn, hold in back; k2; sl p st from cn and p1; k2 from cn.

2/3 LPC – Sl next 3 sts to cn, hold in front; k2; sl p st from cn and p1; k2 from cn.

WRITTEN INSTRUCTIONS TO THE CHART

Row 1 (RS): Inc, k2, p1, [k13, p1], k2, inc.

Row 2 (WS): P3, [k1, p13], k1, p3.

Row 3: Inc, k3, p1, [k13, p1], k3, inc.

Row 4: P4, [k1, p13], k1, p4.

Begin pattern rep:

Row 5: Inc, k2, k2tog, yo, p1, [yo, ssk, k4, p1, k4, k2tog, yo, p1], yo, ssk, k2, inc.

Row 6: P4, k1, [p1, k1, p5, k1, p5, k1], p1, k1, p4.

Row 7: Inc, k2, k2tog, yo, k1, p1, [k1, yo, ssk, k3, p1, k3, k2tog, yo, k1, p1], k1, yo, ssk, k2, inc.

Row 8: P5, k1, [p1, k1, p5, k1, p5, k1] p1, k1, p5.

Row 9: Inc, k2, k2tog, yo, p1, k1, p1, [k1, p1, yo, ssk, k2, p1, k2, k2tog, yo, p1, k1, p1], k1, p1, yo, ssk, k2, inc.

Row 10: P4, k1, p1, k1, [p1, k1, p1, k1, p3, k1, p3, k1, p1, k1], p1, k1, p1, k1, p4.

Row 11: Inc, k2, yo, ssk, k1, p1, k1, p1, [k1, p1, k2, Cable Twist, k2, p1, k1, p1], k1, p1, k1, k2tog, yo, k2, inc.

Row 12: P5, k1, p1, k1, [p1, k1, p1, k1, p3, k1, p3, k1, p1, k1], p1, k1, p1, k1, p5.

Row 13: Inc, k4, yo, ssk, p1, k1, p1, [k1, p1, k2tog, yo, k2, p1, k2, yo, ssk, p1, k1, p1], k1, p1, k2tog, yo, k4, inc.

Row 14: P8, k1, [p1, k1, p5, k1, p5, k1], p1, k1, p8.

Row 15: Inc, k2, p1, k3, yo, ssk, k1, p1, [k1, k2tog, yo, k3, p1, k3, yo, ssk, k1, p1], k1, k2tog, yo, k3, p1, k2, inc.

Row 16: P3, k1, p5, k1, [p1, k1, p5, k1, p5, k1], p1, k1, p5, k1, p3.

Row 17: Inc, k3, p1, k4, yo, ssk, p1, [k2tog, yo, k4, p1, k4, yo, ssk, p1], k2tog, yo, k4, p1, k3, inc.

Row 18: p4, k1, p5, yo, [p3tog, yo, p5, k1, p5, yo] p3tog, yo, p5, k1, p4.

Meet Anna Hunter

ANNA WAS THE VERY FIRST PERSON I EVER MET WHO WAS AN AVID KNITTER AND under the age of fifty. I remember being most impressed by the fact that she could knit anywhere (city bus, dinner party) and not have to look at her needles. Her boyfriend at the time (and now husband) once commented that she was like a spider, just magically creating as she went along. I've known Anna for a number of years now, and she has never stopped creating magic; be it sweaters or hats for her two young boys, or cultivating a space within her yarn shop for other local crafters. – *Amanda*

Where were you born? How long have you lived in BC? What brought you here if you weren't born or raised here?

I was born in Calgary, Alberta, spent a lot of my twenties in Halifax, Nova Scotia, and then moved out to Vancouver in the spring of 2006. I moved here because of a relationship, but found a great job, and sorta fell in love with Vancouver. Then I met my husband, started the shop, and had my kids. Now that I think about it, it's been a very busy seven years.

What is the most inspiring part of BC for you?

I love the landscape; it's breathtaking. My home and shop are both in East Van, so every day no matter where we are, I can look up and see the mountains and look down and see the water. One of my son's first words was *mountains*! Over the years, I have also been inspired by the struggles for social justice that are fought in ways unique to BC, related to housing, poverty, environment, or indigenous rights – it's my other passion (besides knitting of course)!

Who taught you to knit?

When I was 18 I lived in Switzerland as a nanny for a year. During the Christmas holiday we spent some time with the aunt of the kids I took care of. She was a knitter and made these fantastic Austrian sweaters that totally inspired me. I asked her if she could make me one, and she stated that even better than that, she would teach me to make my own. The rest is history!

What was the catalyst that took you from knitting to yarn shop owner? What did you do prior to this or what do you in addition to this as an occupation?

For the decade before I opened the shop, I was working in housing and anti-poverty advocacy work. It is my passion, and I loved the work – but I was burnt out and needed a break. I was on unemployment insurance and trying to figure out the next move. Possibly because I sat on the couch and knitted for two months, my husband suggested I try something with my knitting. This got the wheels turning and I was reminded again that I always longed for an "East Van yarn shop," and then it was like a light turned on and there was no going back. On January 13, 2009, I brought a bottle of champagne home and said, "This is to celebrate that I'm opening a yarn store in East Van," and seven months later Baaad Anna's opened its doors!

Besides the yarn store, I'm a mama to two beautiful boys (aged 3 and 1). I have another small side business called Homesteading Mamas – we teach canning, cheese making, bread baking, and other homesteady type things. I also am very involved in my community and with community-based projects!

What is your favorite part of your job?

The people. I LOVE the community that has been built around the shop. There are almost always a few folks in the shop knitting, talking – sometimes it's about fibre arts and sometimes it's about life, politics, community stuff. But it always feels warm and inviting. The store is a safe place, no matter who you are or what is going on in your life, and that's what I love. Oh yeah – and personally, the fact that my stash is now a big shop is GREAT!

Most useful knitting/crafting tip?

Things are not *always* going to work out. Don't be afraid to rip things out, start again, or embrace the mistakes! Pour yourself a big glass of wine, and start again (maybe that is my biggest piece of life advice too)!

Baaad Anna's has done many things to support the community. Tell us more about your mandate around charity work.

Opening the shop was not only about selling yarn; I wanted my small business to be a responsible, contributing part of my community as well. Every year we do our knit-a-thon, where folks can donate stash yarn, and then for a full day we just knit hats, scarves, mittens, etc., and it's all donated to the Downtown Eastside Women's Centre as part of their holiday hampers. It's a fantastic way for people to give back with something they love.

The community craft rentals was a project we started a year ago to try and make equipment accessible to all people for a very nominal cost. Spinning wheels, looms, drum carders, and more can be rented and used by folks that otherwise wouldn't be able purchase and/or store these things. The response has been great!

Also, our class fees work on a sliding scale where registrants pay based on their income. I also feel it's important to healthy community to support local, so I try to support other small businesses in this industry, whether it is dyers, designers, spinners, etc. I feel this is an essential part of my community mandate!

Any plans for the future?

I want to continue growing our stock of beautiful yarn to knit and crochet with. The shop is also starting to specialize in other fibre arts – spinning, felting, weaving. I'm very excited to see where this will go as more and more people are trying their hand at these other crafts. I also want to continue working with local fibre artists and build an even stronger network of small, local dyers, designers, spinners and businesses.

Meet Holli Yeoh

WE FIRST NOTICED HOLLI AT THE WEST COAST KNITTER'S GUILD MEETINGS. There is a monthly show-and-tell segment that I mustered up the courage to take part in only twice. (It's a big guild! There's a microphone!) Holli, however, would get up every month and have at least three items to show, always her own designs, many for publications. She is the most prolific knitter I have ever known, and the fact that she is constantly turning out new designs at the same time is just amazing to me. She is just full of positive energy, and has always been a great supporter of all of Knit Social's events. We actually had a hard time narrowing down her submissions to include just two in Cascadia. —*Amanda*

What is the most inspiring part of BC for you?

The ocean is what thrills me. I love being at the point where sea meets land. It can be a calm and peaceful meeting or sublimely fierce as the force of the waves crashes against the shore.

Who taught you to knit?

I was five when my mum taught me to knit. That year for Christmas I made potholders for my two grandmothers – one was olive green and the other was orange and brown stripes (it was the '70s!).

What was the catalyst that took you from knitting to design? What did you do prior to this or what do you in addition to this as an occupation?

I've always had a creative bent and graduated with a fine arts degree from the Nova Scotia College of Art and Design. In addition to working at the Vancouver Art Gallery, I designed, made, and taught jewelry.

I knew I wanted to start a family and didn't want to be exposed to the toxins in the jewelry studio. I realized that my passion for knitting could be my creative outlet, so I started designing baby sweaters when I was pregnant with my son.

Most useful knitting/crafting tip?

During critiques, my jewelry instructor in art college always encouraged us to "make ten more." She wanted us to push our boundaries and take our ideas further so that with each successive iteration of the design, we were more likely to come up with something spectacular.

Tell us about your design process.

I find inspiration everywhere. I can often be seen stalking people on the street as I check out their clothes. Sometimes it's the pattern of a tire print in the snow that gets me excited. I often look at stitch patterns for inspiration too.

Once I have an idea of garment shape and stitch pattern, I start swatching. The swatching process can change the original idea completely or it might come out as I first imagined it.

Tell us about your most epic knitting disaster.

I knit a Kaffe Fassett sweater in the early '90s, from a kit. It was a one-size-fits-all design and I did knit a gauge swatch, but it lied. I kept running out of yarn because my sweater was knitting up so much larger than anticipated, but I persevered.

It was so large that the drop shoulders reached my elbows. My sleeves ended up being short, wide wedges. I used to wear a fringed leather jacket underneath the sweater to fill it up. It's now in pieces in a box waiting for me to rework it into something else.

Where is the strangest place you've ever knit?

When I was in my early 20s I travelled around Europe and Africa for six months. Halfway through my trip I desperately wanted a project so I went to the Patricia Roberts shop in London and bought the yarn and pattern for an intricate cabled sweater.

That project came with me to Africa. I was traveling overland on an army vehicle with twelve other people. We camped out at night, cooked our meals over an open fire, and I found myself knitting in temperatures that exceeded 40°C/100°F.

Wake

Holli Yeoh

WITH KNITTING ON MY MIND, I WAS THRILLED TO SEE lacy stitch patterns in the wake behind the BC ferry while going through Active Pass. Every time I rode the ferry I just knew I had to recreate the frothy movement of the water in a sweater design.

The body is worked in one piece to the armholes before dividing to work the fronts and back separately. Waist shaping is achieved by using progressively smaller, then progressively larger needle sizes, creating an unbroken flow of lace to hug the curves. English tailored shoulders and fully-fashioned details finish off the polished, feminine look.

About the Designer

Patterns in the snow, street signs, current fashion, historical dramas – everything is up for grabs when it comes to inspiration. Holli Yeoh views the world through "knit-patterned" glasses. See more of Holli's work at holliyeoh.com or find her on Ravelry as HolliYeoh.

REQUIRED SKILLS

Basic knitting skills; increases/decreases; working simple lace from chart/instructions; knit-on edging; knowledge of basic sweater construction; picking up stitches; seaming; sewing on buttons

SIZES

Women's S (M, L, 1X, 2X); shown in size S

Intended to be worn with zero ease.

FINISHED MEASUREMENTS

Bust: 34¼ (38½, 42¾, 47, 51¼)"

Length from shoulder: 20¾ (21¼, 21¾, 22¼, 22½)"

MATERIALS

SweetGeorgia Yarns Tough Love Sock (80% superwash merino wool, 20% nylon; 425 yds/388m per 115g skein); colour: Hush; 5 (5, 6, 7, 7) skeins

32-inch circular needles in sizes US #3/3.25mm, US #4/3.5mm, US #5/3.75mm, US #6/4mm, or sizes needed to obtain gauge

2 removable stitch markers
8 (9, 9, 10, 10) × ½-inch buttons
2 stitch holders or waste yarn
Yarn needle

GAUGE

19 sts and 27 rows = 4"/10cm in St st with 2 strands of yarn held together, on US #6/4mm needle

19 sts and 28 rows = 4"/10cm in pattern stitch with 2 strands of yarn held together, on US #6/4mm needle, after blocking

PATTERN NOTES

Body is constructed in one piece then divided for armholes.

Waist shaping is achieved through using progressively smaller, then progressively larger needles.

When working shaping in lace patt, be sure that every yarn over is paired with a decrease; if you don't have enough sts to work a decrease, don't work the yarn over. Work rem sts in St st.

Back shoulder shaping is fully fashioned with double decreases, and the front shoulders are worked straight with deeper armholes than the back.

Blocking is best achieved by folding Body piece in half with fronts meeting in the centre.

STITCHES AND TECHNIQUES

K3tog (right-leaning dec): Knit 3 sts tog as one.

Sssk (left-leaning dec): Sl 3 sts kwise one at a time, then knit them tog tbl.

RLI (right lifted inc): Knit into back of st (into the purl bump) in the row/rnd directly below the st on the LH needle.

LLI (left lifted inc): Insert LH needle into back of the st below the st just knitted; knit this st.

PATTERN

Body

With US #5/3.75mm needle, CO 162 (182, 202, 222, 242) sts.

Knit 6 rows. Change to US #6/4mm needle.

Begin stitch pattern:
Row 1 (RS): K1, beg and ending as indicated for your size, work Row 1 of chart, k1.
Row 2 (WS): P1, work Row 2 of chart, p1.

Work in patt as est, maintaining St st selvedge st at each end of row until piece measures 1½ (1¾, 2, 2¼, 2½)" from beg. Change to US #5/3.75mm needle.

Work even until piece measures 3 (3¼, 3½, 3¾, 4)" from beg. Change to US #4/3.5mm needle.

Work even until piece measures 5 (5¼, 5½, 5¾, 6)" from beg. Change to US #3/3.25mm needle.

Work even until piece measures 7 (7¼, 7½, 7¾, 8)" from beg. Change to US #4/3.5mm needle.

Work even until piece measures 9 (9¼, 9½, 9¾, 10)" from beg. Change to US #5/3.75mm needle.

Work even until piece measures 11 (11¼, 11½, 11¾, 12)" from beg. Change to US #6/4mm needle.

Work even until piece measures 13¾ (13¾, 13¾, 13¾, 13¾)" from beg, ending with a RS row.

Divide for fronts and back:
Next row (WS): Working in patt, work 38 (43, 47, 50, 52) sts, BO 5 (5, 7, 11, 17) sts, work 76 (86, 94, 100, 104) sts (including the one leftover from the BO), BO 5 (5, 7, 11, 17) sts, work rem 38 (43, 47, 50, 52) sts. 38 (43, 47, 50, 52) sts each front, 76 (86, 94, 100, 104) sts back.

Place back and left front sts on holders.

Right Front

Armhole shaping:
Refer to Pattern Notes for assistance working decreases in the lace patt.
Dec row (RS): Work to last 4 sts, ssk, k2. 1 st dec'd.

Work dec row every RS row 1 (1, 3, 5, 7) time(s) more. 36 (41, 43, 44, 44) sts.
Work even until armhole measures 5 (5½, 5½, 6, 6½)", ending with a WS row.

Neck shaping:
At neck edge, on RS rows, BO 12 (12, 13, 13, 13) sts once, then 3 sts twice, then 2 sts once, then 1 st twice. 14 (19, 20, 21, 21) sts.

Work even until armhole measures 7 (7½, 8, 8½, 9)", ending with a WS row. Place marker at armhole end of row.

Work even until armhole measures 9 (9½, 10, 10½, 11)", ending with a WS row. Bind off.

Back

Place 76 (86, 94, 100, 104) back sts onto US #6/4mm needle.

With RS facing rejoin yarn.

Armhole shaping:
Dec Row (RS): K2, k2tog, work to last 4 sts, ssk, k2. 2 sts dec'd.
Work Dec Row every RS row 1 (1, 3, 5, 7) time(s) more. 72 (82, 86, 88, 88) sts.
Work even until armhole measures 5 (5½, 6, 6½, 7)", ending with a WS row.

Shoulder shaping:
Double Dec Row (RS): K2, k3tog (see Stitches and Techniques), work to last 5 sts, sssk (see Stitches and Techniques), k2. 4 sts dec'd.
Work Double Dec Row every RS row 2 (7, 8, 9, 8) times more, ending with a WS row. 60 (50, 50, 48, 52) sts.

Single Dec Row (RS): K2, k2tog, work to last 4 sts, ssk, k2. 58 (48, 48, 46, 50) sts.
Work Single Dec Row every RS row 7 (2, 1, 0, 2) time(s) more, ending with a WS row. 44 (44, 46, 46, 46) sts.

Bind off.

Left Front

Place 38 (43, 47, 50, 52) left front sts onto US #6/4mm needle.
With RS facing, rejoin yarn.

Armhole shaping:
Dec row (RS): K2, k2tog, work to end. 1 st dec'd.
Work dec row every RS row 1 (1, 3, 5, 7) time(s) more. 36 (41, 43, 44, 44) sts.

Work even until armhole measures 5 (5½, 5½, 6, 6½)", ending with a RS row.

Neck shaping:
At neck edge (WS rows), BO 12 (12, 13, 13, 13) sts once, then 3 sts twice, then 2 sts once, then 1 st twice. 14 (19, 20, 21, 21) sts.

Work even until armhole measures 7 (7½, 8, 8½, 9)", ending with a WS row. Place marker at armhole end of row.

Work even until armhole measures 9 (9½, 10, 10½, 11)", ending with a WS row. Bind off.

Sleeves

With US #5/3.75mm needle, CO 46 (48, 48, 50, 50) sts.
Knit 6 rows. Change to US #6/4mm needle.

Begin sleeve pattern:
Row 1 (RS): K1, beg and ending as indicated for your size, work Row 1 of chart, k1.
Row 2 (WS): P1, work Row 2 of chart, p1.

Work in patt as est maintaining St st selvedge st at each end of row until sleeve measures 1½" from beg, ending with a WS row.

Inc row (RS): K2, RLI (see Stitches and Techniques), work to last 2 sts, LLI (see Stitches and Techniques), k2. 2 sts inc'd.

Work inc row every 10 (6, 4, 4, 4) rows 2 (2, 0, 6, 14) times more. 52 (54, 50, 64, 80) sts. Work inc row every 12 (8, 6, 6, 6) rows 3 (6, 11, 7, 2) times more. 58 (66, 72, 78, 84) sts.

Work even until sleeve measures 14 (14, 14½, 14½, 15)" from beg, ending with a WS row.

Sleeve cap:
BO 3 (3, 4, 6, 9) sts at beg of next 2 rows. 52 (60, 64, 66, 66) sts.
Double dec row (RS): K2, k3tog, work to last 5 sts, sssk, k2. 4 sts dec'd.
Work double dec row every RS row 1 (6, 6, 4, 1) time(s) more. 44 (32, 36, 46, 58) sts.
Single dec row (RS): K2, k2tog, work to last 4 sts, ssk, k2. 2 sts dec'd.
Work single dec every RS row 8 (2, 4, 9, 15) times more. 26 (26, 26, 26, 26) sts.
Work double dec row every RS row 3 times, ending with a WS row. 14 sts. Bind off.

Finishing

Block pieces to measurements. Sew shaped back shoulder edges to bound-off front shoulder edges.

Neckband

With RS facing and US #4/3.5mm needle, pick up and knit 36 (36, 40, 40, 40) sts along right front neck, 42 (42, 44, 44, 44) sts along back neck, then 36 (36, 40, 40, 40) sts along left front neck. 114 (114, 124, 124, 124) sts.

Knit 5 rows. Bind off.

Buttonband

With RS facing and US #4/3.5mm needle, pick up and knit 102 (104, 104, 107, 108) sts evenly along left front edge from neck opening to bottom edge.

Knit 5 rows. Bind off.

Buttonhole band

With RS facing and US #4/3.5mm needle, pick up and knit 102 (104, 104, 107, 108) sts evenly along right front edge, from bottom edge to neck opening.

Knit 2 rows.

Buttonhole row (WS): K2, [k2tog, yo, k11 (10, 10, 9, 9)] 7 (8, 8, 9, 9) times, k2tog, yo, knit rem 7 (4, 4, 4, 5) sts. 8 (9, 9, 10, 10) buttonholes.

Knit 2 rows. Bind off. Set in sleeves, matching the center of sleeve cap with marker on cardigan front. Sew sleeve and side seams.

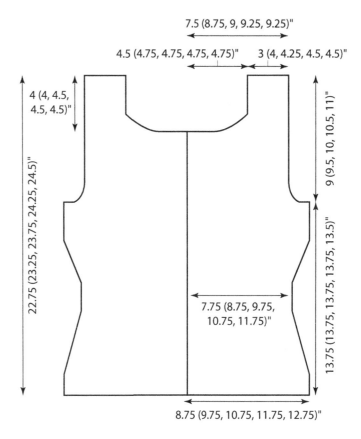

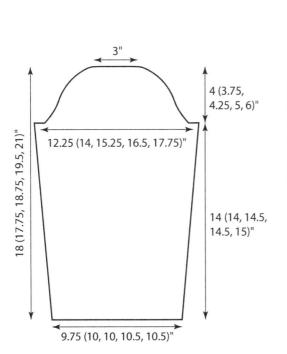

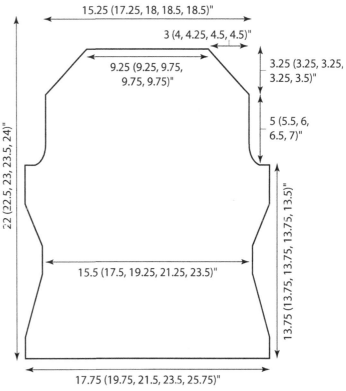

BODY CHART

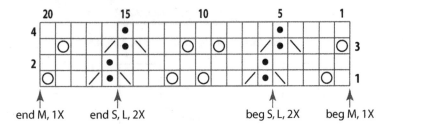

SLEEVE CHART

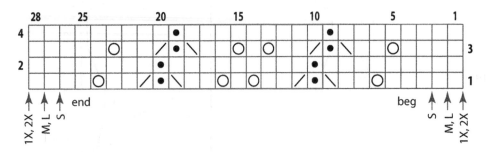

WRITTEN INSTRUCTIONS

Follow either written instructions or charts above.

Body, sizes S, L, 2X only:
(10 st rep worked flat)

Row 1 (RS): [P1, k2tog, k2, yo, k1, yo, k2, ssk] to end.
Row 2 (WS): [P9, k1] to end.
Row 3: [K2tog, k2, yo, k1, yo, k2, ssk, p1] to end.
Row 4: [K1, p9] to end.

Body, sizes M, 1X only:
(10 st rep plus 10 worked flat)

Row 1 (RS): K1, yo, k2, ssk, [p1, k2tog, k2, yo, k1, yo, k2, ssk] to last 5 sts, p1, k2tog, k2, yo.
Row 2 (WS): P4, k1, [p9, k1] to last 5 sts, p5.
Row 3: Yo, k2, ssk, p1, [k2tog, k2, yo, k1, yo, k2, ssk, p1] to last 5 sts, k2tog, k2, yo, k1.
Row 4: P5, [k1, p9] to last 5 sts, k1, p4.

Sleeve, all sizes:
(10 st rep plus 14 (16, 16, 18, 18) worked flat)

Row 1 (RS): K3 (4, 4, 5, 5), yo, k2, ssk, [p1, k2tog, k2, yo, k1, yo, k2, ssk] to last 7 (8, 8, 9, 9) sts, p1, k2tog, k2, yo, k2 (3, 3, 4, 4).
Row 2 (WS): P6 (7, 7, 8, 8), k1, [p9, k1] to last 7 (8, 8, 9, 9) sts, p7 (8, 8, 9, 9).
Row 3: K2 (3, 3, 4, 4), yo, k2, ssk, p1, [k2tog, k2, yo, k1, yo, k2, ssk, p1] to last 7 (8, 8, 9, 9) sts, k2tog, k2, yo, k3 (4, 4, 5, 5).
Row 4: P7 (8, 8, 9, 9), [k1, p9] to last 7 (8, 8, 9, 9) sts, k1, p6 (7, 7, 8, 8).

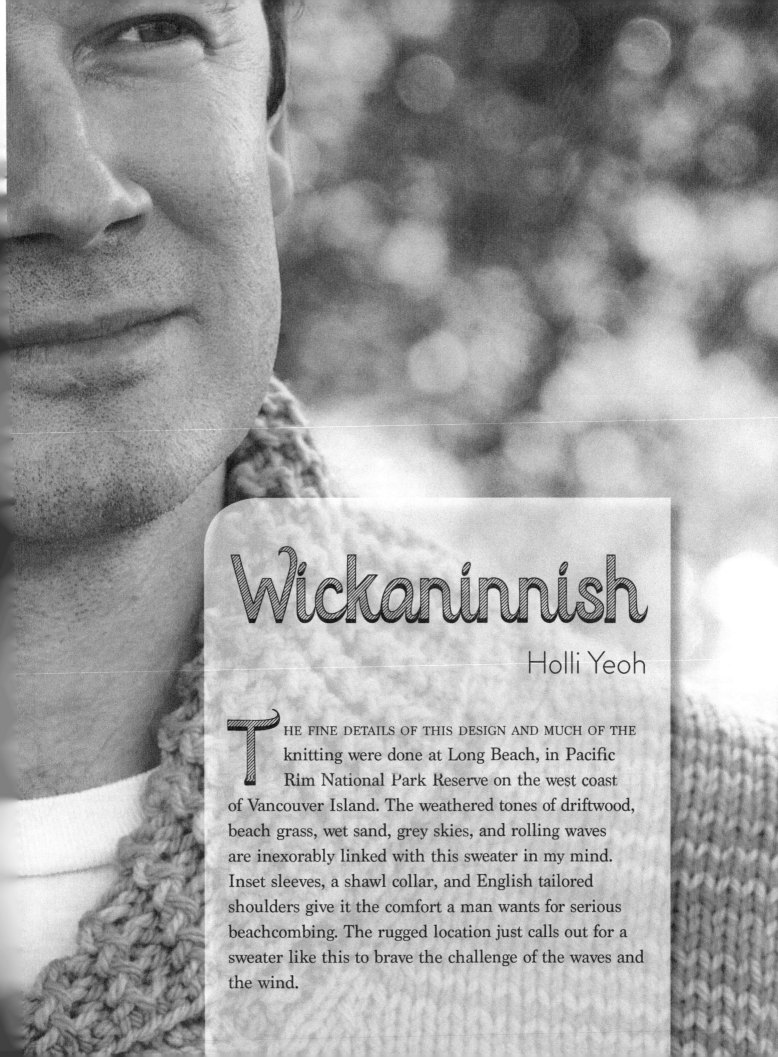

Wickaninnish

Holli Yeoh

THE FINE DETAILS OF THIS DESIGN AND MUCH OF THE knitting were done at Long Beach, in Pacific Rim National Park Reserve on the west coast of Vancouver Island. The weathered tones of driftwood, beach grass, wet sand, grey skies, and rolling waves are inexorably linked with this sweater in my mind. Inset sleeves, a shawl collar, and English tailored shoulders give it the comfort a man wants for serious beachcombing. The rugged location just calls out for a sweater like this to brave the challenge of the waves and the wind.

REQUIRED SKILLS

Basic knitting skills; increases/ decreases; short rows; working simple twisted cable stitches from written instructions; knit-on edging; knowledge of basic sweater construction; picking up stitches; seaming

SIZES

Men's S (M, L, XL, XXL); shown in size M

Intended to be worn with 2–4" positive ease.

FINISHED MEASUREMENTS

Chest: 38¾ (42¾, 46½, 50½, 54¼)"

MATERIALS

Kattikloo Fibre Studio Organic Merino Aran (100% organic merino; 181 yds/166m per 100g skein); color: Metal; 8 (8, 9, 10, 11) skeins

US #7/4.5mm needles
US #8/5mm needles, or size needed to obtain gauge
24-inch US #7/4.5mm circular needle

4 removable stitch markers
Yarn needle

GAUGE

16½ sts and 24 rows = 4"/10cm in St st on US #8/5mm needles

PATTERN NOTES

The English tailored shoulders use double- and triple-cabled decreases to shape the back shoulders. The front shoulders, which have a deeper armhole, are worked straight without shaping and wrap around the tops of the shoulders to the back.

STITCHES AND TECHNIQUES

K3tog: Insert the RH needle into the next three sts on the LH needle simultaneously, as if to knit; knit them tog in 1 st.

Sssk: Slip the next 3 sts, one at a time as if to knit, to the RH needle. Insert the LH needle into the front of these slipped sts and knit all 3 tog in 1 st.

3decB: Triple Cabled Dec Back – transfer 3 sts to cable needle and hold at back, [knit first st on LH needle tog with first st on cable needle] 3 times – 3 sts dec'd.

3decF: Triple Cabled Dec Front – transfer 3 sts to cable needle and hold at front, [knit first st on cable needle tog with first st on LH needle] 3 times – 3 sts dec'd.

2decB: Double Cabled Dec Back – transfer 2 sts to cable needle and hold at back, [knit first st on LH needle tog with first st on cable needle] 2 times – 2 sts dec'd.

2decF: Double Cabled Dec Front – transfer 2 sts to cable needle and hold at front, [knit first st on cable needle tog with first st on LH needle] 2 times – 2 sts dec'd.

T2lk: Twist Two Left Knitwise – reach RH needle behind work, knit through the back lp of second st on needle, leaving sts on needle, knit first st; sl both sts off tog.

T2rp: Twist Two Right Purlwise – purl into second st on needle, leaving sts on needle, purl first st; sl both sts off tog.

Rickrack Ribbing Stitch Pattern: (3-st rep plus 1 worked flat)
Row 1 (RS): P1, [t2lk, p1] to end.
Row 2 (WS): K1, [t2rp, k1] to end.

PATTERN

Back

With smaller needles, CO 82 (90, 98, 106, 114) sts.

Row 1 (RS): [K2, p2] to last 2 sts, k2.

Work in [k2, p2] rib as est until back measures 2" from beg, ending with a WS row.

Knit 4 rows.
Change to larger needles.

Beg with a knit row, work in St st until piece measures 14½ (15, 15, 15, 15¼)" from beg, ending with a WS row.

Armhole shaping:
BO 4 (5, 6, 7, 9) sts at beg of next 2 rows. 74 (80, 86, 92, 96) sts.
Dec Row (RS): K2, k2tog, work to last 4 sts, ssk, k2. 2 sts dec'd.
Work Dec Row every RS row 2 (3, 4, 6, 7) times more. 68 (72, 76, 78, 80) sts.

Work even in St st until piece measures 7 (7½, 8, 8½, 9)" from armhole BO, ending with a WS row.

Shoulder and neck shaping:
Triple dec row (RS): K2, 3decB (see Stitches and Techniques), work to last 8 sts, 3decF (see Stitches and Techniques), k2. 62 (66, 70, 72, 74) sts.
Rep triple dec row every RS row 1 (0, 1, 2, 2) time(s) more. 56 (66, 64, 60, 62) sts.

Double Dec Row (RS): K2, 2decB (see Stitches and Techniques), work to last 6 sts, 2decF (see Stitches and Techniques), k2. 52 (62, 60, 56, 58) sts.
Work Double Dec Row every RS row 6 (8, 7, 6, 6) times more, ending with a WS row. 28 (30, 32, 32, 34) sts.

Bind off.

Fiona Duthie & Kattikloo Fibre Studio

I AM A FIBRE ARTIST, TEACHER, AND DYER AT KATTIKLOO FIBRE STUDIO. I live and work on Salt Spring Island, British Columbia, with my partner and our three boys, but was born in the Shetland Islands, Scotland.

My grandmother is an exceptional Fair Isle knitter and I learned how to knit from her, sitting beside her peat-fired stove in Shetland. My first project was a pair of blue and white Fair Isle mittens, knit in the round. Coming from a place with such a rich textile heritage, it seems inevitable that I would work with wool.

When my first son was born, I began felt making and natural plant dyeing and these have become lifelong obsessions. My aunt in Shetland supplied me with traditional Shetland dyeing books, which were filled with dyeing lore, recipes and the wonderful plant names in Shetland dialect. Kattikloo is one of those traditional dye plant names. I love the connection my craft has with my heritage, and how I interpret the dyes, colours and fibres in my own modern way.

Front

Work as for back until armhole shaping.

Armhole shaping:
BO 4 (5, 6, 7, 9) sts at beg of next 2 rows. 74 (80, 86, 92, 96) sts.
Dec Row (RS): K2, k2tog, work to last 4 sts, ssk, k2. 2 sts dec'd.
Work Dec Row every RS row 2 (3, 4, 4, 4) times more, ending with a RS row. 68 (72, 76, 82, 86) sts.

Sizes S, M and L only:
Work even in St st as required until piece measures 2" from armhole BO, ending with a RS row.

All sizes:
Next row (WS): P40 (42, 44, 48, 50), pm, p28 (30, 32, 34, 36) sts.

Left neck and shoulder shaping:
For sizes XL and XXL, cont to work armhole shaping dec every RS row an additional – (–, –, 2, 3) times while AT THE SAME TIME working neckline decs.

For sizes S, M and L only, armhole shaping is complete and only neckline decs are worked.

All sizes: Next row (RS): Work to marker; turn and work on this set of sts only for left neck shaping. Following row (WS): Purl.

Dec Row (RS): Work to last 4 sts, ssk, k2. 1 (1, 1, 2, 2) sts dec'd; 1 for neckline, 0 (0, 0, 1, 1) for armhole. Work Dec Row every RS row 0 (1, 1, 7, 8) time(s) more. 27 (28, 30, 24, 24) sts. Work Dec Row every 4 (4, 4, 6, 6) rows 7 (7, 8, 1, 1) time(s). 20 (21, 22, 23, 23) sts.

Work even in St st until piece measures 9 (9½, 10, 10½, 11)" from armhole BO. Pm at armhole end of row, then work even until armhole measures 11 (11½, 12, 12½, 13)", ending with a WS row.

Bind off.

Right neck and shoulder shaping: *For sizes XL and XXL only*, cont to work armhole decs on RS rows an additional – (–, –, 2, 3) times while AT THE SAME TIME working neckline decs.

For Size S, M, & L only, armhole shaping is complete and only neckline decs are worked.

All sizes: Next row (RS): Rejoin yarn and BO centre 12 (12, 12, 14, 14) sts, work to end.
Purl 1 row.

Dec Row (RS): K2, k2tog, work to end. 1 (1, 1, 2, 2) sts dec'd; 1 for neckline, 0 (0, 0, 1, 1) for armhole. Work Dec Row every RS row 0 (1, 1, 7, 8) time(s) more. 27 (28, 30, 24, 24) sts. Work dec row every 4 (4, 4, 6, 6) rows 7 (7, 8, 1, 1) time(s). 20 (21, 22, 23, 23) sts.

Work even in St st until piece measures 9 (9½, 10, 10½, 11)" from armhole BO. Pm at armhole end of row, then work even until armhole measures 11 (11½, 12, 12½, 13)", ending with a WS row.

Bind off.

Sleeves

With smaller needles, CO 38 (42, 42, 46, 46) sts.
Row 1 (RS): [K2, p2] to last 2 sts, k2.

Work in [k2, p2] rib as est until sleeve measures 3" from beg, ending with a WS row.

Knit 4 rows.
Change to larger needles.

Sleeve increases:
Inc Row (RS): K2, RLI, knit to last 2 sts, LLI, k2. 2 sts inc'd.
Work Inc Row every 6 (6, 4, 4, 4) rows 8 (7, 5, 3, 8) times more. 56 (58, 54, 54, 64) sts. Work Inc Row every 8 (8, 6, 6, 6) rows 2 (3, 9, 11, 8) times. 60 (64, 72, 76, 80) sts.

Work even until sleeve measures 18 (18½, 19½, 20, 20½)" from beg, ending with a WS row.

Sleeve cap:
BO 4 (5, 6, 7, 9) sts at beg of next 2 rows. 52 (54, 60, 62, 62) sts.

Single Dec Row (RS): K2, k2tog, work to last 4 sts, ssk, k2. 50 (52, 58, 60, 60) sts.
Work Single Dec Row every 4 rows 2 (3, 2, 3, 6) times more. 46 (46, 54, 54, 48) sts. Work Single Dec Row every RS row 12 (12, 16, 16, 13) times. 22 sts.

Double Dec Row (RS): K2, k3tog (see Stitches and Techniques), work to last 5 sts, sssk (see Stitches and Techniques), k2. 18 sts.

Work 1 row even.
Work Double Dec Row once more. 14 sts. Work 1 row even. Bind off.

Finishing

Block pieces to measurements. Sew shaped back shoulder edges to bound off front shoulder edges.

Collar

Notes: RS of collar is worked onto WS of garment because collar is folded over so RS shows when garment is worn. Shawl collar is worked in short rows. At the end of each short row, work a wrap and turn. On the following row, be sure to pick up the wrap and work it tog with st above the wrapped st.

With circular needle and RS facing, start at right corner of centre front neck opening and pick up and knit 38 (40, 42, 45, 47) sts along right edge of neck opening, 28 (30, 32, 32, 34) sts along back neck, then 38 (40, 42, 45, 47) sts along left edge of neck opening – 104 (110, 116, 122, 128) sts. Cut yarn.

Place markers 24 (24, 27, 30, 33) sts from each end of row. 56 (62, 62, 62, 62) sts between markers.

Row 1 (RS of collar): With WS of garment facing, slip sts to first marker. Join yarn, beg Rickrack Rib patt (see Stitches and Techniques) with t2lk (see Stitches and Techniques) and work to second marker, ending with t2lk, remove marker, w&t.

Row 2 (WS of collar): Beg with t2rp (see Stitches and Techniques), work across previous row in Rickrack Rib patt as est to marker, remove marker, work 3 sts; w&t.

Row 3: Beg with t2lk, work to 2 sts beyond previously wrapped st, w&t.

Rows 4 & 5: Work to 0 (0, 2, 2, 2) st(s) beyond previously wrapped st, w&t.

Rows 6 & 7: Work to 1 (1, 2, 2, 2) sts beyond previously wrapped st, w&t.

Rows 8 & 9: Work to 0 (0, 0, 2, 2) st(s) beyond previously wrapped st, w&t.

Rows 10 & 11: Work to 1 (1, 1, 2, 2) sts beyond previously wrapped st, w&t.

Rows 12 & 13: Work to 0 (0, 0, 2, 2) st(s) beyond previously wrapped st, w&t.

Rows 14 & 15: Work to 1 (1, 1, 2, 2) sts beyond previously wrapped st, w&t.

Rows 16 & 17: Work to 0 (0, 0, 0, 2) st(s) beyond previously wrapped st, w&t.

Rows 18 & 19: Work to 1 (1, 1, 1, 2) sts beyond previously wrapped st, w&t.

Rows 20 & 21: Work to previously wrapped st, work wrapped st (tog with its wrap), w&t.

Rows 22 & 23: Work to 1 st beyond previously wrapped st, w&t.

Rows 24 & 25: Work to previously wrapped st, work wrapped st (tog with its wrap), w&t.

Sizes S, M, L only:

Rows 26 & 27: Work to 1 (1, 1, -, -) sts beyond previously wrapped st, w&t.

Rows 28 & 29: Work to previously wrapped st, work wrapped st (tog with its wrap), w&t.

All sizes:

Next row (WS): Work to end of row, CO 1 st. 105 (111, 117, 123, 129) sts.

Next row (RS): Work to end of row, CO 1 st. 106 (112, 118, 124, 130) sts.

Work even in patt as est on all sts until collar measures 7 (7½, 8, 8½, 9)" at centre back, ending with a WS row. BO in a p1, k2 rib.

Sew left front edge of collar (when worn) to centre front BO, lap right front edge behind and sew to BO edge.

Set in each sleeve matching centre of sleeve cap with shoulder marker on front. Sew sleeve and side seams.

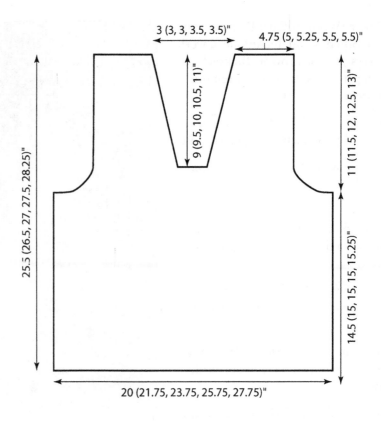

3 (3, 3, 3.5, 3.5)"

4.75 (5, 5.25, 5.5, 5.5)"

9 (9.5, 10, 10.5, 11)"

11 (11.5, 12, 12.5, 13)"

25.5 (26.5, 27, 27.5, 28.25)"

14.5 (15, 15, 15, 15.25)"

20 (21.75, 23.75, 25.75, 27.75)"

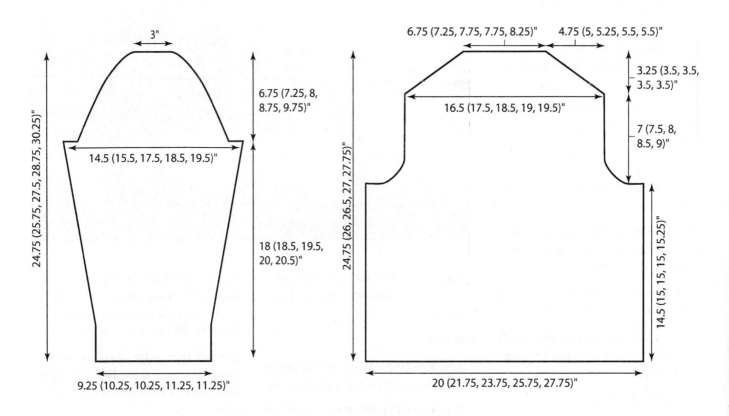

3"

6.75 (7.25, 8, 8.75, 9.75)"

14.5 (15.5, 17.5, 18.5, 19.5)"

24.75 (25.75, 27.5, 28.75, 30.25)"

18 (18.5, 19.5, 20, 20.5)"

9.25 (10.25, 10.25, 11.25, 11.25)"

6.75 (7.25, 7.75, 7.75, 8.25)"

4.75 (5, 5.25, 5.5, 5.5)"

3.25 (3.5, 3.5, 3.5, 3.5)"

16.5 (17.5, 18.5, 19, 19.5)"

7 (7.5, 8, 8.5, 9)"

24.75 (26, 26.5, 27, 27.75)"

14.5 (15, 15, 15, 15.25)"

20 (21.75, 23.75, 25.75, 27.75)"

Meet Melissa Thomson

MELISSA THOMSON HAS BEEN A FRIEND OF KNIT SOCIAL FROM THE EARLY DAYS. We have collaborated with Melissa and Sweet Fiber, her indie company that specializes in luxury hand dyed yarns, at many Knit Social events including our very first retreat. A graduate of the Emily Carr University of Art & Design, Melissa is not only a colour expert but a very talented designer. No Knit Social production would be complete without her and her stunning yarn. —*Fiona*

Where were you born? How long have you lived in BC? What brought you here if you weren't born or raised here?

I was born here in the lower mainland and have lived here for 24 years.

What is the most inspiring part of BC for you?

The most inspiring part of BC for me are the landscapes – the transitions between mountain, ocean, and sky and the colours that go with them. The endless combinations of texture and shapes found here often inspire my knitwear designs. Not to mention the almost always perfect knitting weather.

Who taught you to knit?

My mother taught me to knit the summer after I graduated high school. She had just opened her yarn shop, 88 Stitches, and I suddenly found myself immersed in an unfamiliar yet fascinating world of yarn and knitting. Since then, I've taught myself most of what I know from trial and error as well as online video tutorials.

What was the catalyst that took you from knitting to design? What did you do prior to this or what do you in addition to this as an occupation?

I began designing while in university and at around the same time I started my own hand dyed yarn company, Sweet Fiber Yarns. I am a spatial thinker who enjoys math and figuring things out, so naturally as a knitter I was drawn to knitwear design. Having studied various art mediums and colour theory, I find that the knowledge I gained from those experiences apply directly to knitwear design.

In addition to designing knitwear patterns and hand dyeing yarn, I also work part time and teach classes at 88 Stitches in Langley.

What is your favorite part of your job?

Creating and experimenting. Designing knitwear and hand dyeing yarn allows me to combine my love of knitting, colour, form and function into one activity. I find a lot of creative satisfaction in experimenting with new colours and textures.

Most useful knitting/crafting tip?

Love the materials and tools you use; it makes the entire process more enjoyable.

Tell us about your design process.

My design process begins with a quick burst of inspiration and results in several sketches as I try to capture my visions on paper. After working out a rough pattern, I then cast on right away, ripping out and adjusting as I go. If needed, I make adjustments to the yarn fibre, weight and colour I am using.

Overall I would call my design process organic, as I often allow the design to transform and change as I go through the process of knitting it.

Favorite recent project?

A favorite recent project of mine is the Courtyard Hat I made using merino Twist Worsted in Temperate and Smoke. I really love how the grey sets off the green with the slipped stitch lattice motif.

Tell us about the project you're most proud of.

I've spent the last several months working on my Accessory Collection for Sweet Fiber Yarns. I've had a lot of fun pairing colourways with stitch patterns and creating new cool weather accessories. I'm most proud of this project because I feel it truly embodies who I am as a designer and reflects the natural world where I continuously draw inspiration from.

Where's the strangest place you've ever knit?

The strangest place I have ever knit is on the Vancouver skytrain. Not because it's strange to knit on a train, but because the train can be a very strange place.

Tidal Flats

Melissa Thomson

MIMICKING THE RIVULETS TRAILING THROUGH THE sand at low tide, this cabled hat is perfectly West Coast – practical and simply beautiful. Knit up in a luxurious cashmere blend, Tidal Flats is the perfect stylish-yet-cozy slouchy toque.

REQUIRED SKILLS

Knitting in the round; decreases; long-tail cast on; cabling

SIZES

Sized to fit head circumferences: 22 (24)"

FINISHED MEASUREMENTS

Circumference: 19 (21)"
Depth: 9 (9)"

MATERIALS

Sweet Fiber Yarns Cashmerino Worsted (80% superwash merino, 10% cashmere, 10% nylon, 200 yds/183m per 115g skein); shown in Winter, 1 skein.

16-inch US #5/3.75mm circular needle
16-inch US #7/4.5mm circular needle, or size needed to obtain gauge

1 set US #7/4.5mm needles for working small circumferences in the round: dpns, 1 long circular or 2 short circulars

1 removable stitch marker
Cable needle
Yarn needle

GAUGE

18 sts and 29 rnds = 4"/10cm over St st on larger needles, blocked

STITCHES AND TECHNIQUES

3/3 RC - Sl next 3 sts to cn, hold in back; k3, then k3 from cn.

3/3 LC - Sl next 3 sts to cn, hold in front; k3, k3 from cn.

3/2 RCp - Sl next 2 sts to cn, hold in back; k3, then p2 from cn.

2/1 LCp - Sl next 3 sts to cn, hold in front; p1, k3 from cn.

3/1 RCp - Sl next st to cn, hold in back; k3, p1 from cn.

3/2 LCp - Sl next 3 sts to cn, hold in front; p2, then k3 from cn.

3/3 RCp - Sl next 3 sts to cn, hold in back; k3, then p3 from cn.

3/3 LCp - Sl next 3 sts to cn, hold in front; p3, k3 from cn.

PATTERN

Using smaller needle, CO 88 (96) sts. Place marker and join for working in the rnd.

Ribbing: [K1, p1] around. Work Ribbing as est until piece measures 2 (2)" from CO edge.

Change to larger circular needle.

Set-up Rnd: K4, pm, k1, p10, k6, p4, k6, p10, k1, pm, knit to end of rnd. Work the Set-up Rnd twice more.

Body Rnd: Knit to marker, work Cable Pattern (see chart) over next 38 sts, knit to end of rnd.

Work as est until all 28 rows of cable patt are complete, then work Rows 1-14 once more.

Crown Decreases

Note: Work crown decreases between markers only.

Crown Rnd: Knit to marker, work Decrease Chart over next 38 sts, knit to end of rnd.

Work as set until all 11 rows of cable patt are complete. 60 (68) sts.

Rnd 12: K2tog twice, ssk twice, p2tog, k2tog to end of rnd. 30 (34) sts.
Rnd 13: K2tog around. 15 (17) sts.

Cut yarn leaving a long tail, thread the tail through the rem sts, pull tight and secure on wrong side. Block, then weave in ends.

About the Designer

Melissa Thomson is the creative director of Sweet Fiber Yarns, as well as a knitwear designer. She lives in Langley, BC.

38   35   30   25   20   5   1

28
27
26
25
24
23
22
21
20
19
18
17
16
15
14
13
12
11
10
9
8
7
6
5
4
3
2
1

k – knit

p – purl

3/1 LCp – Sl next 3 sts to cn, hold in front; p1, k3 from cn.

3/1 RCp – Sl next st to cn, hold in back; k3, p1 from cn.

3/2 LCp – Sl next 3 sts to cn, hold in front; p2, then k3 from cn.

3/2 RCp – Sl next 2 sts to cn, hold in back; k3, then p2 from cn.

3/3 LC – Sl next 3 sts to cn, hold in front; k3, k3 from cn.

3/3 RC – Sl next 3 sts to cn, hold in back; k3, then k3 from cn.

DECREASE CHART

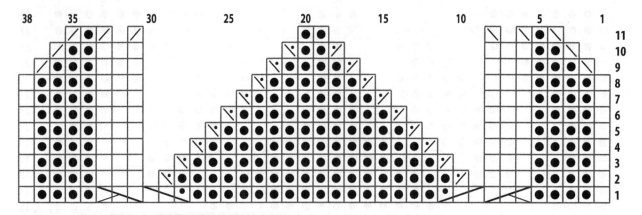

	k – knit
●	p – purl
╱	k2tog – knit 2 together
╲	ssk – slip, slip, knit
╱	p2tog – purl 2 together
╲	p2tog – purl 2 together tbl
	3/3 RCp – Sl next 3 sts to cn, hold in back; k3, then p3 from cn.
	3/3 LCp – Sl next 3 sts to cn, hold in front; p3, k3 from cn.

Meet Caitlin ffrench

Everybody loves Caitlin ffrench. Her talent and enthusiasm for natural dyeing, coupled with her exuberant personality and style, have made her somewhat of a celebrity in the Vancouver fibre community and beyond. She forages in the forest for her dyeing materials, makes her own mordants, and dries her hand-dyed yarn on her front porch. She sews and hand-writes on each and every one of her ball bands. This dedication to her craft is impressive to say the least, and we can't wait to see what she accomplishes next. —*Fiona*

What is We Will Tell You All Of Our Secrets?

We Will Tell You All Of Our Secrets is the name of my textile art studio, natural dye adventures, and blog. I make one-of-a-kind colourways using both exotic dyes and plants that I forage for or source locally. I also design knitting patterns under the same name.

What is the story behind the name?

It came from my thoughts around knowledge sharing. I really think that people hold their secrets too close because they don't want others to be able to do what they do. I love when people tell me that they are interested in natural dyes. I want to help other people get excited about discovering pigment! I want others to do what I do. Running around the forest or walking around the city and knowing which plants will yield colour is brilliant!

I am also terrible at keeping secrets. I really have a hard time with them, especially keeping secrets about myself.

Where are you from originally?

I am from the Okanagan region, and grew up on the same orchard in Oyama that my mother was raised on and still lives on today.

What is your background in the fibre arts? How did you get started with natural dyeing?

When I was much younger, my mom taught me to sew and my Oma tried to teach me to knit. A dear friend re-taught me to knit in my early 20s on our way to a punk rock show.

I also went to the Kootenay School of the Arts to study fibre arts. They have a great program and I learned how to naturally dye there. Being a natural dyer is much like being an alchemist. My front porch is covered with jars of yarns and fibres that are solar dyeing, and my neighbors poke fun at me and call me a witch, which I take as a huge compliment.

I am also a weaver, spinner, knitter, crocheter, and I sew the majority of my own clothes. (If only to make clothing that properly fits my six-foot-tall frame).

Tell us more about your foraging for dye materials, and your favourite dye methods.

As of late, about 80 percent of what I do is with dyes I collect from the forest or from my home and garden. In the Okanagan I also have my mom growing flowers for me, and there is a walnut tree at her house where I collect hulls. My favorite natural dye is walnut husks from this tree. It is HUGE, and was planted when she was young. Now every year we collect the husks for me to dye with. It was the tree I used to hang out in as a kid, so it is great that I can still be close to it even though I live far away.

I also have a huge affinity for onion skins. It makes such a striking orange-yellow with an alum mordant, and a rich green with iron as a mordant.

My favorite dye method is stove-top dyeing with an iron mordant. It makes the richest, darkest colours.

What inspires you?

I am inspired by so much. My partner is my greatest love, and my harshest critic. Having someone not only telling you what you're doing right, but also telling you when you need to change what you're doing is a huge asset. We met at school (UBC–Okanagan) where we were both completing our fine arts degrees. Being able to work (we paint and build sculptures together, and he assists me with dye collection and dyeing) alongside each other inspires me to work harder all of the time.

I'm also inspired by my home surroundings. The colours that exist here year-round are a big part of my life. I listen to a lot of ambient noise and doom metal when harvesting dyes, and it brings more clarity to what I consider to be a meditative process. Remembering to thank the land when you go out harvesting, and taking only what you need are things that I always keep in mind.

What other projects do you have on the go?

I am growing a flax garden for the Urban Cloth Project. There are many of us around Vancouver growing large and small fields of flax. Most of us have not done it before, so we are all learning together.

We are going to be harvesting the flax plants in the fall, and turning them into spin-able linen fibre. We are then going to weave the linen into cloth, and make clothing. I think this is a brilliant project. We are literally growing our clothes!

Meet Amanda Kaffka

I FIRST MET AMANDA KAFFKA AT URBAN YARNS IN VANCOUVER. I DIDN'T KNOW EXACTLY what I was looking for at the store, but I had a vague plan that I was going to knit matching cardigans for my four nieces. Despite the distraction of my then-one-year-old crawling around our feet and yanking yarn off the shelf, she helped me pick out the perfect pattern and yarn for the project. Her patience and eye for colour combinations really impressed me and I have been following her design career since. We are thrilled to include her beaded Sea Glass Pullover in the *Cascadia* collection. —*Fiona*

Where were you born? How long have you lived in BC? What brought you here if you weren't born or raised here?

I was born in Aurora, Oregon. I came to Vancouver with my mom when I was about four years old and I have been living in BC ever since.

Who taught you to knit?

My mom taught me to knit when I was six, on Pender Island. She made me a pair of arbutus-twig knitting needles, and the rest is history. I expanded my knowledge by choosing patterns that were always too hard for me.

What was the catalyst that took you from knitting to design? What did you do prior to this or what do you in addition to this as an occupation?

I have always been interested in design. I have a fashion design degree from Ryerson University in Toronto, which taught me the foundations of design for fabric execution.

After graduation I dabbled in the industry briefly but wasn't truly satisfied. Leaving fashion for about five years, I worked for a graphics and photography company in the hotel and tourism industry, then later started a baby accessory business with a friend that fulfilled my design side for a while until I realized it was not my passion.

It wasn't until I seriously picked up my knitting needles again and found the Vancouver knitting community that I truly felt like I had found purpose and passion. I currently work at my LYS, Urban Yarns, where I teach kid's, adult-beginner and beyond-beginner classes and design whenever I have the chance.

Tell us about your design process.

I am always inspired by yarns, colours, street wear, and shapes. I constantly have designs in my head and it's just about sketching them out and finding the time to knit. I love fashion and keeping up with the latest trends whether it be knitwear, fabric, accessories, ready-to-wear, couture or colour.

I don't necessarily design what's in trend; I like to mix it up, finding new shapes, and I love mixing textures. I design what I want to wear and what I think my audience will find wearable.

Tell us about your most epic knitting disaster.

A woman came into the shop with a sweater her mother had started before she passed away and wanted me to finish it. I agreed to do the work (knitting and seaming) and also teach her how to knit again. For about four months I taught this woman one or two times per week and really got to know her, and we established a great friendship.

In the meantime I worked on the sweater here and there. It was made of this chunky weight 100% cotton that was super heavy and stiff to work. When it was time to block it, I soaked the sweater and laid it out to dry. The next day I checked on it and it had started to mould – the cream sweater was now turning yellow. I quickly washed the sweater again and thought I would put it in front of my mini fireplace to dry faster but within hours it was starting to mould again. I washed the sweater a third time and out of desperation put it in the dryer. I took it out of the dryer and there was no mould, but now it had shrunk!

I took the sweater to my student/friend and told her what had happened and after taking the sleeves off to try to salvage the sweater to a wearable state I looked at her with pleading eyes and said, "Your mother didn't want this sweater finished, she wanted us to connect and for you to get back into knitting." We had a good laugh over it, thank goodness!

Where is the strangest place you've ever knit?

I bring my knitting everywhere; some friends and family say my knitting is my security blanket... maybe they are right. I can't bear the thought of sitting in a car or waiting for a bus or at an appointment without my knitting.

I personally don't think it is strange to knit anywhere, so I think if I were to ask my friends/family where the strangest place they have seen me knit is, it would have to be in the middle of a party and maybe at a funeral reception.

Sea Glass

Amanda Kaffka

Sea Glass is a simple, chunky lace knit with beaded detail on the front. Worked in the round until the underarms and only seamed at the shoulders, this simply constructed pullover is the perfect quick knit. The oversized boxy style can be worn casually over a pair of jeans or shorts, or dressed up over skinny pants or a skirt. Inspired by the ease and calm of collecting sea glass on our local BC beaches next to the waves, the beads add a subtle elegance and interest. Make one in neutrals with monochromatic beads, or try bold colours with flashy or sparkly beads.

About the Designer

Amanda Kaffka learned to knit on arbutus twigs at age six and hasn't looked up since. She's been caught knitting at traffic lights, bars and beaches, but her backyard is her favourite place.

REQUIRED SKILLS

Knitting in the round; increases/decreases; beading knit-wise; knitted cast on or cable cast on; three-needle bind off; tubular bind off; working simple lace from chart and/or written instructions; knowledge of basic sweater construction; picking up stitches

SIZES

Girl's 6–8 (Women's S, M, L)

Intended to be worn with 2" of positive ease

FINISHED MEASUREMENTS

Bust: 29 (44, 51, 59)"

Length: 11 (18, 21, 28)" from shoulder

MATERIALS

SweetGeorgia Chunky (100% merino wool; 120yds/109m per 100g skein); 2(4, 5, 6) skeins. Shown in Jade (M sample), Tumbled Stone (S sample), Saffron (Girls sample)

24-inch US #8/5mm circular needle
16-inch US #8/5mm circular needle
24-inch US #10/6mm circular needle, or sizes needed to obtain gauge

2 stitch markers in contrasting colours
16 (36, 49, 72) × 8-10mm beads (make sure chunky yarn can fit through hole)
0.6mm crochet hook or dental floss threader, for beading
Stitch holder or waste yarn
Yarn needle

GAUGE

12 sts and 14 rnds = 4"/10 cm in St st, on larger needle blocked

PATTERN NOTES

The Sea Glass pullover is knit in the round from the bottom to the underarm, then the back and front are worked flat and separately to the shoulder. It starts with a broken rib and then goes into a simple lace pattern. Place beads on the front of the pullover only between the markers. (It is optional to place beads on the back as well; please note bead count will double). Knit all stitches when working on Rows 11 and 21 while working on the back stitches.

STITCHES AND TECHNIQUES

Place Bead: remove next st from left needle and thread bead onto st. Place st back onto left needle and knit the st with the bead on.

Broken rib pattern (over a multiple of 2 sts, worked in the rnd):
Rnd 1: [K1, p1] around.
Rnd 2: Knit around.

Tubular Bind Off
Thread yarn tail onto yarn needle.
Set-up Step 1: Insert the yarn needle into the first st on the LH needle purlwise, pull yarn through and leave the st on the needle.
Set-up Step 2: Going behind the first st on the LH needle, insert yarn needle into the second st on the LH needle knitwise, pull yarn through and leave the st on the needle. (This can be slightly awkward).
Step 1: Insert yarn needle into the first st on LH needle knitwise, taking st off. (Do not pull yarn all the way through.)
Step 2: Insert yarn needle into the second st on the LH needle purlwise, pull yarn through both sts.
Step 3: Insert yarn needle into the first st on needle purlwise, taking st off. (Do not pull yarn all the way through.)

Step 4: Going behind the second st on the LH needle, insert yarn needle into the second st on the LH needle knitwise, leaving the st on the needle, and pull the yarn through both sts. (This can be slightly awkward.)

Rep Steps 1–4 until you have bound off all your sts.

[See this video tutorial for further help: www.knittinghelp.com/video/play/tubular-bind-off]

PATTERN

Lower Body

With 24-inch US #8/5mm needles, CO 88 (132, 154, 176) sts using long tail cast on. Place marker A and join in the rnd, taking care not to twist.

Work in broken rib patt (see Stitches and Techniques) for 2 (2½, 2½, 3)", ending with Rnd 1 of the patt.

Change to 24-inch US #10/6mm needles.

Body rnd: Work Lace patt (from chart or written instructions as you prefer; see Stitches and Techniques) around starting on Rnd 10, placing a marker after 44 (66, 77, 88) sts to divide the front and back.

Note: Beads are only placed on the first 44 (66, 77, 88) sts in Rnds 11 and 21.

Cont in Lace patt, working rows as foll for your size: 10–22 & 1–11 (10–22 & 1–21; 10–22 & 1–22 & 1–11; 10–22 & 1–22 & 1–21). You will now have 3 (4, 5, 6) rows of beads.

Divide front & back

Start working flat, back and front separately, removing markers on the first row. Follow flat patt chart without adding beads on rows 11 and 21 for the back.

Upper Back

Row 1 (WS): CO 1 st at beg of row, p1, work 44 (66, 77, 88) back sts starting at row 12 (22, 12, 22) of flat chart, turn. 45 (67, 78, 89) sts.

Row 2 (RS): CO 1 st at beg of row, k1, work 44 (66, 77, 88) sts in patt as set, k1, turn.

Slip the rem sts to a holder. These will be used later for the front.

Back row 3 (RS): K1, work 44 (66, 77, 88) sts in patt as set to marker, k1.

Back row 4 (WS): P1, work 44 (66, 77, 88) sts in patt as set to marker, p1.

Cont in patt as est – working patt Rows 11 & 21 without beads – until you have completed the following rows, as per your size: 12–21 (22 & 1–21; 12–22 & 1–11; 22 & 1–22 & 1–11).

Knit 6 (10, 10, 12) rows.

Next row, create shoulders (WS): Knit 14 (20, 24, 28) sts, then slip them to a holder. BO 18 (28, 31, 34) center sts, knit to end of row. Slip last 14 (20, 24, 28) sts of the row to a holder. Break yarn.

Upper Front

Return 44 (66, 77, 88) held sts of front to needle. With WS facing, rejoin yarn, and work as foll:

Row 1 (WS): CO 1 st at beg of row, p1, work 44 (66, 77, 88) front sts starting at row 12 (22, 12, 22) of flat chart, turn. 45 (67, 78, 89) sts.

Row 2 (RS): CO 1 st at beg of row, k1, work 44 (66, 77, 88) sts in patt as set, k1, turn. 46 (68, 79, 90) sts.

Front Row 3 (RS): K1, work 44 (66, 77, 88) sts in patt as set to marker, k1.

Front Row 4 (WS): P1, work 44 (66, 77, 88) sts in patt as set to marker, p1.

Cont in patt as set – working patt Rows 11 & 21 with beads – until you have completed the following rows, as per your size: 13–21 (2–21; 13–22 & 1–11; 2–22 & 1–11)

You will now have 4 (6, 7, 9) rows of beads.

Knit 6 (10, 10, 12) rows.

Next row, create neck opening (WS): K14 (20, 24, 28) sts, then slip them to a holder. BO 18 (28, 31, 34) center sts, knit to end of row.

Following row (RS): K 14 (20, 24, 28), and slip these sts to a holder. Break yarn and rejoin to start of other set of live sts, with RS facing. Knit across them, and leave on needle – do not break yarn.

Seam shoulders: Place back right shoulder sts back on needle. Hold with right sides tog, and use US #8/5mm needle to work 3-needle BO across sts. Break yarn. Place back left shoulders sts onto needles. Hold with right sides tog and using tail from back shoulder sts, work 3-needle BO.

Finishing

Block piece to final measurement according to schematic before continuing.

Once blocked, pick up and knit around armholes (both left and front alike: Using 16-inch US #8/5mm needles with RS facing starting at the underarm, pick up and knit 12 (26, 26, 34) sts to shoulder, 12 (26, 26, 36) back to underarm. 24 (42, 42, 68) total sts. Place marker and work broken rib for 2 (4, 4, 6) rnds.

Break yarn leaving a tail that is at least 3 times the length of the circumference of your armhole. Bind off using Tubular Bind Off method (see Stitches and Techniques).

Weave in ends.

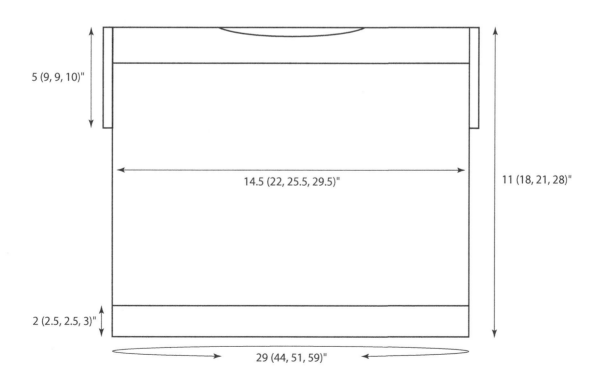

5 (9, 9, 10)"

14.5 (22, 25.5, 29.5)"

11 (18, 21, 28)"

2 (2.5, 2.5, 3)"

29 (44, 51, 59)"

LACE CHART
(WORKED IN THE ROUND)

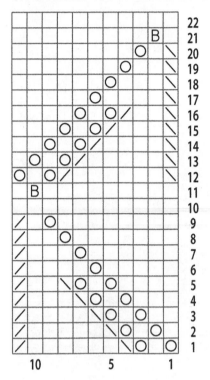

LACE CHART
(WORKED FLAT)

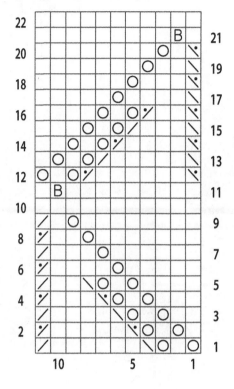

☐ **k** – knit on RS, purl on WS

O **yo** – yarn over

╱ **k2tog** – knit 2 together

╲ **ssk** – slip, slip, knit

B **place bead**

⟋ **p2tog** – purl 2 together

⟍ **p2tog tbl** – purl 2 together tbl

WRITTEN INSTRUCTIONS

Lace Pattern worked in the round

Multiple of 11 sts. Work either chart above or written instructions below.

Rnd 1: [Yo, k1, yo, ssk, k6, k2tog] around.
Rnd 2: [K1, yo, k1, yo, ssk, k5, k2tog] around.
Rnd 3: [K2, yo, k1, yo, ssk, k4, k2tog] around.
Rnd 4: [K3, yo, k1, yo, ssk, k3, k2tog] around.
Rnd 5: [K4, yo, k1, yo, ssk, k2, k2tog] around.
Rnd 6: [K5, yo, k4, k2tog] around.
Rnd 7: [K6, yo, k3, k2tog] around.
Rnd 8: [K7, yo, k2, k2tog] around.
Rnd 9: [K8, yo, k1, k2tog] around.
Rnd 10: Knit.
Rnd 11: [K9, place bead, k1] around.
Rnd 12: [Ssk, k6, k2tog, yo, k1, yo] around.
Rnd 13: [Ssk, k5, k2tog, yo, k1, yo, k1] around.

Rnd 14: [Ssk, k4, k2tog, yo, k1, yo, k2] around.
Rnd 15: [Ssk, k3, k2tog, yo, k1, yo, k3] around.
Rnd 16: [Ssk, k2, k2tog, yo, k1, yo, k4] around.
Rnd 17: [Ssk, k4, yo, k5] around.
Rnd 18: [Ssk, k3, yo, k6] around.
Rnd 19: [Ssk, k2, yo, k7] around.
Rnd 20: [Ssk, k1, yo, k8] around.
Rnd 21: [K1, place bead, k9] around.
Rnd 22: Knit.

Lace Pattern worked flat

Multiple of 11 sts. Work either chart above or written instructions below.

Row 1 (RS): [Yo, k1, yo, ssk, k6, k2tog] to end.
Row 2 (WS): [P2tog, p5, p2togtbl, yo, p1, yo, p1] to end.
Row 3: [K2, yo, k1, yo, ssk, k4, k2tog] to end.
Row 4: [P2tog, p3, p2togtbl, yo, p1, yo, kp] to end.
Row 5: [K4, yo, k1, yo, ssk, k2, k2tog] to end.

Row 6: [P2tog, p4, yo, p5] to end.
Row 7: [K6, yo, k3, k2tog] to end.
Row 8: [P2tog, p2, yo, p7] to end.
Row 9: [K8, yo, k1, k2tog] around.
Row 10: Purl.
Row 11: [K9, place bead, k1] to m; knit to end.
Row 12: [Yo, p1, yo, p2tog, p6, p2togtbl] to end.
Row 13: [Ssk, k5, k2tog, yo, k1, yo, k1] to end.
Row 14: [P2, yo, p1, yo, p2tog, p4, p2togtbl] to end.
Row 15: [Ssk, k3, k2tog, yo, k1, yo, k3] to end.
Row 16: [P4, yo, p1, yo, p2tog, p2, p2togtbl] to end.
Row 17: [Ssk, k4, yo, k5] to end.
Row 18: [P6, yo, p3, p2togtbl] to end.
Row 19: [Ssk, k2, yo, k7] to end.
Row 20: [P8, yo, p1, p2togtbl] to end.
Row 21: [K1, place bead, k9] to m; knit to end.
Row 22: Purl.

Meet Amanda Milne

I AM GRATEFUL, PRETTY MUCH ON A DAILY BASIS, THAT AMANDA IS MY BUSINESS PARTNER. She has the rare qualities of being both incredibly organized and wonderfully creative. Rather than finding that intimidating (which it is), I find it inspirational. The beauty of our partnership is that we motivate each other to do our best rather than compete with each other, and I think that's pretty special. I can't imagine running Knit Social with anyone else. Above all else though, she is my dear friend, and I am super proud of her design for this book. —*Fiona*

Where were you born? How long have you lived in BC? What brought you here if you weren't born or raised here?

I was born in Chilliwack, BC, at the same hospital my father was. I lived there until I was 20, when I packed up and moved to North Vancouver with my boyfriend at the time. From there I moved to Vancouver, where I met my husband and we've been here ever since.

What is the most inspiring part of BC for you?

The fact that it has always been my home, yet I can still be awed by it. The landscape, in its many forms as you travel from the coast into the Okanagan, is so familiar to me but still so wild. I don't know if I could live anywhere where I didn't have as much access to water as I do here. It's quite humbling, living beneath the mountains and next to the Pacific Ocean.

Who taught you to knit?

Anna Hunter of Baaad Anna's taught me to knit while I was pregnant with my first child. She herself had not yet opened her yarn shop, but was such a passionate and creative knitter that it really made an impression on me and encouraged me to persevere through miles of very, very poor garter stitch.

Most useful knitting/crafting tip?

Don't let impatience win out over properly planning out your projects. Now ask me if I take my own advice....

Tell us about your most epic knitting disaster.

Not necessarily one project, but rather a series of them. When I first began knitting I made hats, primarily. I was pretty proud that I had figured out the whole knit in the round deal, and found them a lot more interesting to knit than scarves or blanket squares.

I didn't really pay much attention to gauge though. I made my husband a series of hats, five or six of them, and not one of them fit properly. Not one. It was ridiculous. He was very kind about it, but still looks a little wary if I ever ask if he wants a new hat.

Tell us about the project you're most proud of.

A Fair Isle sampler scarf. The design idea isn't mine, but every block of fair isle I knit in the scarf was of my own choosing (patterns and colours) and I did design a few blocks myself too. It has my children's names and my wedding date knit into it, and I absolutely cherish it.

What's the strangest place you've ever knit?

I don't think it's all that strange, but people do tend to look at you funny when you knit in a bar.

Heather

Amanda Milne

HEATHER IS A SIMPLE LACE-PANELED TOQUE WITH A fetching curved garter brim. Wear it down low for a cloche-like style, or farther back for a slouchy look. Using a light fingering-weight yarn held doubled ensures a luscious squish and helps to smooth out the appearance of hand-dyed yarns that might show too much variegation or pooling otherwise.

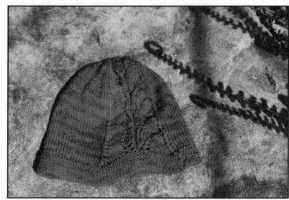

REQUIRED SKILLS

Basic knitting skills; knitting in the round; knitting with double-pointed needles; increases/decreases; working simple lace from chart or written instructions

SIZES

Sized to fit head circumferences: 21 (22½)".

FINISHED MEASUREMENTS

Circumference: 19 (20½)"
Depth: 8½ (9)"

MATERIALS

Indigo Moon Yarns BFL Light Fingering (100% Blue-faced Leicester superwash wool, 430 yds/393m per 100g skein); color: Wild Berries; 1 (1) skein

About the Designer

Amanda Milne is one half of Knit Social Event Co. She lives in Vancouver, BC, with her husband and two children. Heather is her first published pattern.

Note: Yarn is held doubled throughout.

16-inch US #6/4mm circular needle
US #6/4mm dpns, 1 long circular or 2 short circulars, or size needed to obtain gauge

Yarn needle
Stitch markers

GAUGE

21 sts and 32 rnds = 4"/10cm in St st with yarn held doubled

STITCHES AND TECHNIQUES

Sk2p: Slip 1 st purlwise from LH needle, knit next 2 sts tog, pass slipped st over the 2 sts knit tog.

PATTERN

Using circular needle, CO 104 (112) sts, using the long-tail method. Pm and join for working in the rnd, being careful not to twist sts.

Brim

Rnd 1: Purl.
Rnd 2: Knit.
Rep these 2 rnds 5 (7) more times for a total of 6 (8) garter ridges.

Body

Rnd 1: Work Fern Lace Pattern Chart A over next 28 sts, pm, knit to end of rnd.
Work as set until 4 full repeats of Fern Lace Pattern A are complete.

Crown Decreases

You'll work Fern Lace Pattern Chart B (see Stitches and Techniques) and decreases in the plain section.

Rnd 1: Work Chart B; k6 (14), k2tog, [k15, k2tog] 4 times. 97 (105) sts.
Rnds 2, 4, 6, 8, 10: Work Chart B, knit to end of rnd.
Rnd 3: Work Chart B; k5 (13), k2tog, [k14, k2tog] 4 times. 90 (98) sts.
Rnd 5: Work Chart B; k4 (12), k2tog, [k13, k2tog] 4 times. 83 (91) sts.
Rnd 7: Work Chart B; k3 (11), k2tog, [k12, k2tog] 4 times. 76 (84) sts.
Rnd 9: Work Chart B; k2 (10), k2tog, [k11, k2tog] 4 times. 69 (77) sts.
Rnd 11: Work Chart B; k1 (9), k2tog, [k10, k2tog] 4 times. 62 (70) sts.

Lace Chart B ends. Cont working as foll:

Size S only:

Rnd 12: K2tog, k5, p2, k5, k2tog twice, [k9, k2tog] 4 times. 57 sts.

Rnd 13: K2tog, k4, p2, k4, k3tog, [k8, k2tog] 4 times. 50 sts.
Rnd 14: K2tog, k3, p2, k3, k2tog, [k7, k2tog] 4 times. 44 sts.

Rnd 15: K2tog, k2, p2, k2, k2tog, [k6, k2tog] 4 times. 38 sts.
Rnd 16: K2tog, k1, p2, k2, k2tog, [k5, k2tog] 4 times. 32 sts.

Rnd 17: K2tog around. 16 sts.
Rnd 18: K2tog around. 8 sts.

Size L only:

Rnd 12: K2tog, k5, p2, k5, k2tog, k8, k2tog, [k9, k2tog] 4 times. 65 sts.
Rnd 13: K2tog, k4, p2, k4, k2tog, k7, k2tog, [k8, k2tog] 4 times. 58 sts.

Rnd 14: K2tog, k3, p2, k3, k2tog, k6, k2tog, [k7, k2tog] 4 times. 51 sts.
Rnd 15: K2tog, k2, p2, k2, k2tog, k5, k2tog [k6, k2tog] 4 times. 44 sts.

Rnd 16: K2tog, k1, p2, k1, k2tog, k4, k2tog, [k5, k2tog] 4 times. 37 sts.
Rnd 17: K2tog, p2, k2tog, k3, k2tog, [k4, k2tog] 5 times. 30 sts.

Rnd 18: K2tog around. 15 sts.
Rnd 19: K2tog to last st, k1. 8 sts.

Finishing

Thread tail through rem sts, pull tight and weave in ends.

Trish Moon & Indigo Moon Yarns

USING ONLY EXQUISITE SILKS AND THE SOFTEST MERINO WOOLS FOR dyeing, I draw on the colours of my garden and the forest around me. The resulting yarn palette is rich and jewel-like, yet muted and infused with earth tones. I use a technique that has taken years to create: my yarns are hand-dyed over an open flame, and I use the minerals found in the well water to impart an earthy cast to all Indigo Moon Yarns.

Throughout the year, I work dyeing yarns for crafters to use in creating their own works of art. This time is punctuated by weaving commissions: Winter Meditation shawls, Commemoration Blankets woven to celebrate the life of loved ones, and OM Blankets woven to surround a person with healing energy during a long illness.

Dyed and woven in limited quantities by hand to keep them exclusive, Indigo Moon Yarns are rich, beautiful, and positively West Coast.

FERN LACE PATTERN A

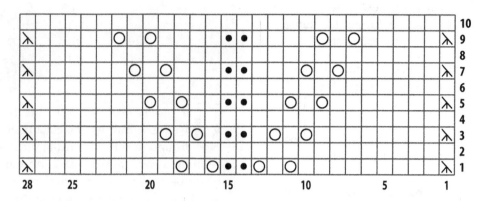

	k – knit
●	p – purl
O	yo – yarn over
\	ssk – slip, slip, knit
/	k2tog – knit 2 together
⊠	sl1, k1, psso – slip 1, k1, pass slipped st over
⋋	sk2p – slip 1, k2tog, pass slipped st over

FERN LACE PATTERN B

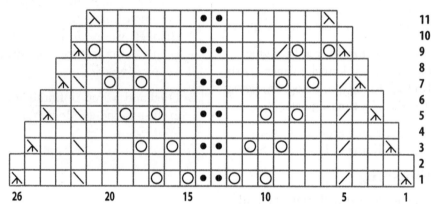

WRITTEN INSTRUCTIONS

Fern Lace Pattern A

Worked in the round over 28 sts.

Rnd 1: Sk2p, k9, yo, k1, yo, p2, yo, k1, yo, k9, sk2p.
Rnd 2: Knit.

Rnd 3: Sk2p, k8, yo, k1, yo, k1, p2, k1, yo, k1, yo, k8, sk2p.
Rnd 4: Knit

Rnd 5: Sk2p, k7, yo, k1, yo, k2, p2, k2, yo, k1, yo, k7, sk2p.
Rnd 6: Knit.

Rnd 7: Sk2p, k6, yo, k1, yo, k3, p2, k3, yo, k1, yo, k6, sk2p.
Rnd 8: Knit.

Rnd 9: Sk2p, k5, yo, k1, yo, k4, p2, k4, yo, k1, yo, k5, sk2p.
Rnd 10: Knit.

Fern Lace Pattern B

Worked in the round over 28 sts.

Rnd 1: Sk2p, k3, k2tog, k4, yo, k1, yo, p2, yo, k1, yo, k4, ssk, k3, sk2p. 26 sts.
Rnd 2: Knit.

Rnd 3: Sk2p, k2, k2tog, k3, yo, k1, yo, k1, p2, k1, yo, k1, yo, k3, ssk, k2, sk2p. 24 sts.
Rnd 4: Knit.

Rnd 5: Sk2p, k1, k2tog, k2, yo, k1, yo, k2, p2, k2, yo, k1, you, k2, ssk, k1, sk2p. 22 sts.
Rnd 6: Knit.

Rnd 7: Sk2p, k2tog, k1, yo, k1, yo, k3, p2, k3, yo, k1, yo, k1, ssk, sk2p. 20 sts.

Rnd 8: Knit.

Rnd 9: Sk2p, yo, k1, yo, k2tog, k3, p2, k3, ssk, yo, k1, yo, sk2p. 18 sts.
Rnd 10: Knit.

Rnd 11: Skp, k6, p2, k6, skp. 16 sts.

Abbreviations

approx	approximately
beg	beginning
BO	bind off
cn	cable needle
CO	cast on
cont	continue
dec('d)	decrease(d)
dpn(s)	double-pointed needle(s)
est	established
foll	following
inc('d)	increase(d)
k	knit
kwise	knitwise
LH	left hand
lp(s)	loop(s)
p	purl
patt	pattern
pm	place marker
rem	remain(ing)
rep	repeat
rnd(s)	round(s)
RH	right hand
RS	right side
set	established
sl	slip
sm	slip marker
st(s)	stitch(es)
St st	stockinette stitch
tbl	through the back loop
tog	together
w&t	wrap and turn
WS	wrong side
yo	yarn over

Resources

Amanda Kaffka
knittyknittygritty.wordpress.com/about

Baaad Anna's
baaadannas.wordpress.com

Cascade Yarns
www.cascadeyarns.com

Everything Old
everything-old-crafts.blogspot.ca

Holli Yeoh
www.holliyeoh.com

Indigo Moon
www.indigomoonyarns.com

Jane Richmond
www.janerichmond.com

Judy Marples
purlbumps.wordpress.com

Kattikloo Fibre Studio
www.kattikloo.com

Kim Werker
kimwerker.com

Knit Social
knitsocial.ca

Megan Goodacre
www.megangoodacre.com

nook.
inanook.blogspot.ca

Ravelry
www.ravelry.com

Sweet Fiber Yarns
sweetfiberyarns.com

SweetGeorgia Yarns
www.sweetgeorgiayarns.com

Tin Can Knits
www.tincanknits.com